Speaking Out: Researching and Representing Women

CONTENTS

Who's Who and Where's Where:
Constructing Feminist Literary Studies
Mary Eagleton — 1

Situated Voices:
'Black Women's Experience' and Social Work
Gail Lewis — 24

Insider Perspectives or Stealing the Words Out of Women's Mouths:
Interpretation in the Research Process
Diane Reay — 57

Revolutionary Spaces:
Photographs of Working-class Women by Esther Bubley 1940–1943
Jacqueline Ellis — 74

Between Identification and Desire:
Rereading *Rebecca*
Janet Harbord — 95

Poem:
Daisy, Rose and Lily
Claire Nicol — 108

Reviews

Norma Clarke on *Becoming a Woman and Other Essays in 19th and 20th Century Feminist History* — 109

Erica Burman on *Antisemitism, Misogyny and the Logic of Cultural Difference: Cesare Lombroso and Matilde Serao* — 111

Claire Alexander on *New Right Discourse on Race and Sexuality: Britain 1968–1990* — 113

Jane K. Cowan on *Alcohol, Gender and Culture*

Peggy Watson on *Gender Politics and Post-Communism: Reflections from Eastern Europe and the Former Soviet Union; Cinderella Goes to Market: Citizenship, Gender and Women's Movements in East Central Europe* **119**

Rosalind Gill on *Straight Sex: the Politics of Pleasure* **122**

Wendy Hollway on *Rethinking Sexual Harassment* **125**

Marie-Claude Foster and **Susan F. Murray** on *Medicine and Nursing. Professions in a Changing Health Service* **127**

Letter **130**

Noticeboard **131**

Feminist Review is published three times a year. It is edited by a collective which is supported by a group of corresponding editors.

The Collective: Avtar Brah, Ann Phoenix, Annie Whitehead, Catherine Hall, Dot Griffiths, Gail Lewis, Helen Crowley, Merl Storr.

Corresponding Editors: Ailbhe Smyth, Ann Curthoys, Hala Shukrallah, Kum-Kum Bhavnani, Jacqui Alexander, Lidia Curti, Patricia Mohammed, Sue O'Sullivan.

Guest Editors for Issue 52: Ann Curthoys, Helen Irving, Jeannie Martin.

Correspondence and advertising
Contributions, books for review and editorial correspondence should be sent to: Feminist Review, 52 Featherstone Street, London EC1Y 8RT.
For advertising please write to:
Journals Advertising, Routledge, ITP Journals,
2–6 Boundary Row, London SE1 8HN, UK.

Subscriptions
Please contact Routledge Subscriptions Department, Cheriton House, North Way, Andover, Hants SP10 5BE, UK. Tel: 44 (0)1264 342713; Fax 44 (0)1264 342807; E-mail debby.shaw@ITPS.co.uk. A full listing of Routledge books and journals is available by accessing http://www.routledge.com/routledge.html

Notes for Contributors
Authors should submit four copies of their work to: *Feminist Review*, 52 Featherstone Street, London EC1Y 8RT. We assume that you will keep a copy of your work. Submission of work to *Feminist Review* will be taken to imply that it is original, unpublished work, which is not under consideration for publication elsewhere.
All work is subject to a system of anonymous peer review. All work is refereed by at least two external (non-Collective) referees.

Bookshop distribution in the USA
Routledge, 29 West 35th Street, New York, NY 10001, USA.

Typeset by Type Study, Scarborough
Printed in Great Britain by Bell & Bain Ltd, Glasgow

Copyright © 1996 in respect of the collection is held by *Feminist Review*.
Copyright © 1996 in respect of individual articles is held by the authors.

PHOTOCOPYING AND REPRINT PERMISSIONS
Single and multiple photocopies of extracts from this journal may be made without charge in all public and educational institutions or as part of any non-profit educational activity provided that full acknowledgement is made of the source. Requests to reprint in any publication for public sale should be addressed to the *Feminist Review* at the address above.

ISSN 0141-7789

The *Feminist Review* office has moved.
Please send all correspondence to:
Feminist Review
52 Featherstone Street
London EC1Y 8RT

Who's Who and Where's Where:
Constructing Feminist Literary Studies

Mary Eagleton

Abstract

This article is concerned with the construction of feminist literary studies in the last twenty years and points out how we have created a literary history which is both selective and schematic. It suggests that we should be more critically aware of what we are constructing, how we are constructing it and of the political consequences of those constructs. It stresses three critical modes which might help us to complicate our history: a greater awareness of institutional contexts, a concern with empirical detail, and an ongoing analysis of the cultural and political significance of feminist literary practice. This article briefly applies these critical modes in a survey of eleven introductions to feminist literary studies – introductions which feature frequently and influentially in the teaching situation. The final section focuses on the key problem of inclusion and exclusion. Considering arguments from Third World feminism and postmodernist feminism, the study concludes that white, academic feminists should confront the privilege of their own inclusion as a necessary spur to political action.

Keywords

feminist literary history; feminist literary theory; feminist teaching; empiricism; location; the *supplément*

Introduction

> The past presents itself to us, always, somehow simplified. He wants to avoid that fatal unclutteredness, but knows he can't.
> (Mukherjee, 1994: 6)

> Before you build another city on the hill, first fill in the potholes at your feet.
> (Mukherjee, 1994: 91)

In many feminist and women writers' classes I have told the story of feminist literary theory, as Catherine Belsey and Jane Moore say, 'the story so far' (1989: 1–20). First there was Virginia Woolf. Then came

1968 with its explosion of political activity across Europe and the United States, including what became known as 'Women's Lib'. A cluster of significant texts was produced about that time: Tillie Olsen's 'Silences' (1965), an essay in *Harpers Magazine* which later became a collection of interconnected essays under the same title (1980); Mary Ellmann's *Thinking About Women* (1968); two popular texts partly concerned with women's depiction in literature and language, Eva Figes's *Patriarchal Attitudes* (1970) and Germaine Greer's *The Female Eunuch* (1970); and the most renowned of them all, Kate Millett's *Sexual Politics* (1970). By the late 1970s some of the founding texts and key names of feminist literary criticism were established: Patricia Meyer Spacks's *The Female Imagination* (1976); Ellen Moers's *Literary Women* (1978); Elaine Showalter's *A Literature of Their Own* (1978), and Sandra Gilbert and Susan Gubar's *The Madwoman in the Attic* (1979). At the same time voices of discontent could be heard concerning the predominant whiteness and heterosexuality of the emerging feminist literary debates: for instance, Barbara Smith's 'Toward a black feminist criticism' (1977); Adrienne Rich's 'Compulsory heterosexuality and lesbian existence' (written in 1978; first published in 1987); Deborah McDowell's 'New directions for black feminist criticism' (1980), and Bonnie Zimmerman's 'What has never been: an overview of lesbian feminist criticism' (1981). The 1980s seem to have been dominated by 'the French' and the impact of post-1968 theoretical work which, by then, had found its way from the Continent to American and British universities. In particular, postmodernist thought led to a revaluation of all the categories that feminists had held both dear and true: identity, woman, feminist, history, progress, collectivity. At this point, I review the history of socialist and radical feminisms as a counter to the more rarefied, less politicized aspects of postmodernism. As the story moves into the 1990s I usually end with a few pluses and minuses – the welcome advent of Third World feminisms; the important insights from psychoanalytic feminism; continuing concern about the loss of a central emphasis on class, and the hope for a re-emergence of a strongly political feminist criticism, attentive to postmodernist debates but with a renewed sense of political purpose. Then a mental bell rings in the back of my brain and I begin to wind up.

As a cursory look at volumes of feminist literary theory and critical practice will indicate, this is a familiar narrative and yet for me it is one that is becoming increasingly difficult to offer without numerous reservations and qualifications. Large sections of the account now need to be placed within imaginary inverted commas as the received version but a highly questionable one. For instance, what is the justification for seeing Virginia Woolf as origin, as if feminist criticism suddenly and miraculously sprang fully formed from her pen? Certainly there is no justification within Woolf herself. She argues in *A Room of One's Own* (1929):

> masterpieces are not single and solitary births; they are the product of many years of thinking in common, of thinking by the body of the people, so that the experience of the mass is behind the single voice.
>
> (Woolf, 1929; 1933; 1993: 59–60)

Then, too, why the curious gap between the death of Woolf and 1968? This is sometimes filled with an aside to Simone de Beauvoir's *The Second Sex* (1949; 1953, English translation), which features as a kind of solitary beacon, keeping feminism alight in the dark days of the 1950s but related only marginally in most accounts to either French or American feminism of the post-1968 period.[1] Germaine Greer, too, has always maintained an uneasy relationship with the major narrative of feminist criticism, positioned and positioning herself in an isolated role as both icon and iconoclast.

What about the other feminisms I mention: black, lesbian, Third World? Therein lies the problem. In most versions of this narrative they remain precisely that, 'other', defined *in relation to* the dominant white, heterosexual account, an interesting adjunct, an intervention that momentarily arrests the white and/or heterosexual reader into self-critical thought. Notice, for instance, my phrase 'the welcome advent of Third World feminisms'. How my words betray me. It is not Third World feminism that has just come into existence; rather the change lies in a recent and belated willingness on the part of the First World academic to recognize Third World feminism. And why did I choose the word 'advent' – an arrival, a coming – if I wasn't at some level thinking of Third World feminism as entering and adding to an already established corpus? And why did I collectively group together under the title 'voices of discontent' very different forms of feminism that have taken issue in different ways with a hegemonic feminism which is itself differentiated? The deconstructive role which white/heterosexual feminism frequently offers to black, Third World and lesbian feminisms to undermine white, heterosexual norms exhibits an openness to criticism which is in part illusory. The 'other' feminisms are restricted to a reactive mode, almost, in some ways, a servicing function in supplying the missing chapters to the dominant story, as if they have nothing to say about and for themselves. In this context Trinh T. Minh-ha illustrates how 'difference' is transposed into 'division', becoming 'no more than a tool of self-defense and conquest' (Trinh, 1989: 82).

In reassessing the history of feminist literary thought, one would want to question how the post-1968 account of literary feminism came to be a tale of theoretical positions, a tale of '-isms'. At its most irritating was that period when every new book title seemed to be a medley of words in inverted commas, slashes, hyphens, words with bracketed syllables, puns, coinages, question marks – all asserting the playfulness of language and the instability of any identity. Self-consciously quagmired in theory, unable to say anything guilelessly about anything, how one longed for a title such as *A Book About Women's Writing*. Equally, the frequency with which certain narrative structures repeat themselves needs examination. Sometimes the story of literary feminism features as a kind of *Bildungsroman* from naïvety to sophistication, from the innocently experiential to theoretical density. The history is progressive, purposeful, history ever onwards and upwards. On other occasions we replicate literary Oedipal narratives where the son tries to kill his critical father. In our case adversarial oppositions are 1970s versus 1990s, Anglo-American versus French, radical versus poststructuralist – fading mothers and less than dutiful daughters. Then again, binary oppositions can give way to a sense of our history as movements; each wave brings with it a further exploration, more subtle perceptions, adding to or refuting the earlier knowledge. Considerable academic status is associated with 'newness', to be at the cutting edge, conversant with the most modish names and vocabulary. Recently a vein of nostalgia has crept into some narrations; the story has become a lament for past certainties, for a golden age of clarity and activism.

In formulating our arguments or in demarking our history feminists, as often as anyone else, are in the grip of a form of numerology. Discussion is frequently specifically structured around *two* texts or authors in conjunction or opposition or *one* text or author as given and the other as supplement. For example, one version of the history is to place Woolf and de Beauvoir alongside each other as founding mothers to the generation of 1968 (Todd, 1988; Belsey and Moore, 1989) or Millett and Ellmann as 'classic' voices of 1968 (Moi, 1986). Another is to place Woolf and Showalter in opposition (Moi, 1986) and subsequently Showalter and Moi in opposition (Eagleton, 1991). Whether our history is told in terms of time shifts, political positions or forms of critical thought, there are never more than three or four elements. Sometimes the historical periods are in decades – 1970s, 1980s, 1990s – though, as we move into the twenty-first century, decades will become too small a unit to be operable and some reordering of the figures will soon be required. Sometimes we deal in 'phases' which are sequential but not necessarily linked to decades. With an absolutism she has probably come to regret, Elaine Showalter claims in *A Literature of Their Own* (1978: 13): 'In looking at literary subcultures, such as black, Jewish,

Canadian, Anglo-Indian, or even American, we can see that they *all go through three major phases*' (my italics). The history of women writers as a subculture, she explains, passes through the three phases of 'Feminine', 'Feminist' and 'Female'. Elizabeth Grosz, examining feminist thoughts, generally sees 'three decades' (1960s, 1970s, 1980s), corresponding to 'three phases' ('sexist, patriarchal, and phallocentric') and producing 'three distinct kinds of response' (liberal feminism, conservative feminism, radical feminism) (Grosz, 1987). Julia Kristeva, in 'Women's time', characterizes three 'generations' of feminists (Kristeva, 1979; 1981, English translation). It will not have escaped your notice that, here, I have given three examples.

What is lost in these accounts is a sense of confusion and indeterminacy, the cacophony of voices and views, the uncertain currency of any idea, the unevenness of history. The sheer mass of experience gives way to a severe streamlining, as Mukherjee says in my epigraph, the 'fatal unclutteredness' with which we remember the past, or, as Trinh comments, 'the reconstruction and redistribution of a pretended order of things, the interpretation or even transformation of documents given and frozen into monuments' (Trinh, 1989: 84). I am not suggesting, even if it were feasible, that feminists should give up historical records and drift into some unstructured continuum or that we should leave the recording to others; we have been too long 'hidden from history' for that. Nor am I suggesting that with a bit of effort feminism could produce a complete history with a place for everything and everything in its place. What I am questioning is the schematic form of these records and how the process of selecting, ordering, prioritizing is both controlling and deeply ideological. Chela Sandoval, thinking about the place – or lack of place – of US Third World feminism, comments on 'the official stories by which the white woman's movement understands itself and its interventions in history' and how these stories serve to 'legitimize certain modes of culture and consciousness only to systematically curtail the forms of experiential and theoretical articulations permitted U.S. third world feminism' (Sandoval, 1991: 5–6). Sandoval's comments could obviously be related to the position of other marginal groups and, though I accept her protest about the restraining effect of the 'white woman's movement', even within that movement the emphasis on 'three phases', 'three distinct kinds of response', 'three generations', hardly points to a generous pluralism.

Yet as I say this I also understand the reasons that lead feminists to this kind of skeletal history and I am all too aware of my complicity in this restricted story-telling in my own teaching and writing and, at the same time, of the inevitability of that complicity. There is no uncontaminated space, non-ideological, egalitarian, unthreatened by power differentials, in which the story can be fully and honestly told; there is no way of offloading the inequities of history and starting afresh. The primary demand from my students for their courses and for the few books they can afford to purchase is for a synopsis of 'the story so far'. The student coming new to this area understandably wants to hear some rapid contextualizing of the major names, titles and issues; she wants to be familiar with 'the official stories', what she believes every other feminist knows. I appreciate that expectation while feeling that it often locks me into the repeated production of a kind of feminist Great Tradition and into retellings of a history about which I now have so many caveats and hesitancies that it is difficult to discern any narrative shape at all. Sometimes I look with a jaundiced eye at the introductions to feminist literary theory that I have produced and see them as a desperate act of containment in the face of the proliferating numbers of women writers, feminisms, other critical theories, course modules, the size of student groups – all the product of a specific historical moment in British higher education and academic publishing.

What I want to advocate in this article is a greater sensitivity to how we are constructing our feminist critical history and more thought about the meanings of what we are creating. As indicated above, one requisite would be an understanding of institutional contexts and demands and the wider political and economic forces that situate them. For example, there has been very little analysis of the development of feminist publishing and the part that location has played in determining feminist thought, or of the surreal experience in recent years of practising a feminine/feminist literary discourse in institutions which are becoming increasingly phallocentric and 'managerialized'. (For what it's worth, I am now adept at translating the concepts of *l'écriture féminine* into four neat learning outcomes, three modes of assessment and a near-guaranteed twenty credit points.) Second, I would welcome a renewed emphasis on empirical detail: who, when, where, which publications and journals, which conferences, which networks, what database, what was translated, into which languages? In an age obsessed with detail as information retrieval it is something of a cultural paradox that detail as literary history is so difficult to find. An interest in the empirical does not necessarily signify, in Peggy Kamuf's words, 'an unshaken faith in the ultimate arrival at essential truth through the empirical method of accumulation of knowledge, knowledge about women' (Kamuf, 1982: 45). But it may provide necessary information neglected by grander forms of system building in contemporary theory. 'Before you build another city on the hill, first fill in the potholes at your feet' (Mukherjee, 1994: 91). Such detail would help us to trace the movements of feminist literary history and would be the essential preliminary for a third activity, the analysis of the cultural and political significance of important figures, events and artefacts.

In what follows I should like to use these modes of critical approach with reference to two areas. First, to look at a range of introductions to feminist literary theory and practice to see how they construct the standard version of literary feminism: who's who in feminist literary studies? Second, to consider the geography of literary feminism, what world it has encompassed: where's where in feminist literary studies? Through such analysis we might find ways of opening out the dominant narrative and in those specific spaces where feminist theory and criticism lives – taking part in a seminar, writing an essay, compiling a book list – we (teachers, students, readers and writers of feminist literary studies) might begin to upset the feminist orthodoxies. Finally, I want to focus on a problem which introductory collections, readers, surveys, because of their form, raise with particular sharpness; namely, the problem of inclusion and exclusion.

Who's who in feminist literary studies

First, then, a little modest empirical work. I examined eleven introductions to feminist literary theory and practice, concentrating on texts which feature on introductory reading lists, and hence often constitute a student's first and formative meeting with feminist criticism. I aimed to cover an historical spread (1979–1996) and to look at texts produced on both sides of the Atlantic but all available in Britain.[2] The texts are as follows:

> 1979 – Jacobus, Mary (ed.), *Women Writing and Writing about Women* London and Sydney: Croom Helm;
> 1982 – Abel, Elizabeth (ed.), *Writing and Sexual Difference* Chicago: University of Chicago Press;
> 1985 – Greene, Gayle and Kahn, Coppélia (eds), *Making a Difference: Feminist Literary Criticism* London: Methuen;
> 1985 – Newton, Judith and Rosenfelt, Deborah (eds), *Feminist Criticism and Social Change* London: Methuen;
> 1985 – Moi, Toril, *Sexual/Textual Politics: Feminist Literary Theory* London: Methuen;
> 1986 – Showalter, Elaine (ed.), *The New Feminist Criticism* London: Virago;
> 1989 – Belsey, Catherine and Moore, Jane (eds), *The Feminist Reader: Essays in Gender and the Politics of Literary Criticism* London: Macmillan;
> 1991 – Eagleton, Mary (ed.), *Feminist Literary Criticism* London: Longman;

1991 – Warhol, Robyn and Price Herndl, Diane (eds), *Feminism: An Anthology of Literary Theory and Criticism* New Brunswick, New Jersey: Rutgers University Press;
1994 – Humm, Maggie, *A Reader's Guide to Contemporary Feminist Literary Criticsm* London: Harvester Wheatsheaf;
1996 – Eagleton, Mary (ed.), *Feminist Literary Theory: A Reader* (second edn.) Oxford: Blackwell.

Who constitutes literary feminism?[3] The following critics appear in five or more of the texts above (number given in parentheses):

Susan Gubar (7)	Abel, Moi, Showalter, Belsey, Warhol, Humm, Eagleton (1996).
Elaine Showalter (7)	Jacobus, Abel, Moi, Showalter, Eagleton (1991), Warhol, Eagleton (1996).
Hélènë Cixous (6)	Moi, Belsey, Eagleton (1991), Warhol, Humm, Eagleton (1996).
Sandra Gilbert (6)	Moi, Showalter, Belsey, Warhol, Humm, Eagleton (1996).
Mary Jacobus (6)	Jacobus, Abel, Belsey, Eagleton (1991), Warhol, Eagleton (1996)
Cora Kaplan (6)	Jacobus, Greene, Newton, Eagleton (1991), Warhol, Eagleton (1996).
Julia Kristeva (6)	Moi, Belsey, Eagleton (1991), Warhol, Humm, Eagleton (1996).
Gayatri Spivak (6)	Abel, Belsey, Eagleton (1991), Warhol, Humm, Eagleton (1996).
Ann Rosalind Jones (5)	Greene, Newton, Showalter, Warhol, Eagleton (1996).
Annette Kolodny (5)	Abel, Moi, Showalter, Warhol, Eagleton (1996).
Barbara Smith (5)	Newton, Showalter, Warhol, Humm, Eagleton (1996).
Bonnie Zimmerman (5)	Greene, Showalter, Warhol, Humm, Eagleton (1996).
Featuring in four: Luce Irigaray.	In three: Michèle Barrett, Catherine Belsey, Barbara Christian, Rosalind Coward, Rachel Blau DuPlessis, Shoshana Felman, Paul Lauter, Kate Millett, Ellen Moers, Toril Moi, Lillian Robinson, Catharine Stimpson.

These texts are not aiming at comprehensiveness: Newton and Rosenfelt's collection specifically concentrates on materialist–feminist criticism; Toril Moi's study defines two main strands in feminist criticism, the Anglo-American and the French, and sticks to them; even Maggie Humm's commendably extensive survey is 'by no means a full portrait' (Humm, 1994: ix). But the texts must be aiming to include, at least, the significant or salient; there would be little point in focusing on material which the author or editor then dismisses as inconsequential. The list illustrates that literary feminism regularly confirms the status of significance on no more than a dozen names and that status is reaffirmed with similar frequency in the many general introductions to critical theory which invariably name feminist literary studies such as Showalter, Gilbert, Gubar, Cixous. . . . The base becomes even narrower when one looks at the particular works chosen to represent the author; not only a dozen key names but no more than a dozen or so key texts. For Showalter, the likely choice is 'Toward a feminist poetics' (1979) or 'Feminist criticism in the wilderness' (1981); for Spivak, 'French feminism in an international frame' (1981) or 'Three women's texts and a critique of imperialism' (1985). For Kolodny, the most frequent choice is 'Dancing through the minefield: some observations on the theory, practice, and politics of a feminist literary criticism' (1980); for Cixous, 'The laugh of the Medusa' (1976), closely followed by an extract from 'Sorties: out and out: attacks/ways out/forays' (1986); for Kristeva, 'Women's time' (1981). Zimmerman's 'What has never been: an overview of lesbian feminist criticism' (1981) was selected by all her anthologizers, and Jones's 'Writing the body: toward an understanding of *l'écriture féminine*' (1981) by all except Greene and Kahn, who make use of another introduction to French feminism by Jones, 'Inscribing femininity: French theories of the feminine' (1985); Smith's 'Toward a black feminist criticism' (1977) was used by all anthologizers except Warhol and Price Herndl.

The essays have acquired specific roles in the unveiling saga of feminist literary theory. Showalter's 'Toward a feminist poetics' is the *locus classicus* for the definition of 'gynocriticism', itself a distinctive mode in American literary feminism. Kolodny's summary of the state of play at the end of the 1970s became a model for many future essays: on the one hand, looking back to see how far we've come (again history by decades); on the other, looking around to see how we've held our own in the war of the theories. Certain essays and authors have attained a metonymical function with reference to particular critical positions: Smith's relation to black feminism; Zimmerman and lesbian feminism; Kaplan and Marxist-feminism; Jacobus, at least the later Jacobus, and psychoanalytic feminism. Showalter's 'Feminist criticism in the wilderness' and Jones's 'Writing the body: toward an understanding of *l'écriture féminine*' take up the task of interpreting, almost accommodating French feminism to an American audience. Spivak's positioning is particularly interesting, not only as the messenger from France (translator of Derrida's *Of Grammatology* (1976) and hugely knowledgeable about European thought) but also the voice of the Third World and the subaltern: 'French Feminism in an International Frame' conjoins the two perspectives. In retrospect we can see how the essays both create the moment, conceptualize it in a certain way for future readers and how they are created by the moment, a product of a particular history. We can see how meanings have continued to circulate and accrue around these pivotal figures and texts, some clinging tenaciously like barnacles, others more readily disgarded.

Where's where in feminist literary criticism

On the basis of this list of key texts the geography of feminist literary thought and the world literary feminism constructs as its territory seem equally delimited. The pre-eminence of American born and/or based critics is one of the striking factors about our galaxy of 'stars'. Gubar, Showalter, Gilbert, Kaplan, Jones, Kolodny, Smith, Zimmerman, are all American by birth and working in America, though Kaplan taught for many years at the University of Sussex and produced the material that is often anthologized while working in Britain. Jacobus is British by birth, taught at Oxford but now teaches at Cornell. Spivak is Indian by birth, did her graduate work at Cornell and has since taught at American universities. To explain in institutional and cultural terms the centrality of the United States in the production of feminist literary criticism would involve, at least, a consideration of the history of civil rights and liberation politics; of the developed infrastructure of women's studies programmes in universities, feminist journals and publishing houses, distribution networks, well-endowed libraries, the availability of grants and scholarships; of the gravitational pull which the United States holds for feminist academics around the world; of the pressure to publish so as to gain tenure or promotion, a pressure which has affected women's studies as much as any other discipline.

It is only in the three citations category that the British critics begin to feature: Michèle Barrett is included in Newton, Humm and Eagleton (1996); Catherine Belsey in Newton, Warhol and Eagleton (1996) and Rosalind Coward in Showalter, Belsey and Eagleton (1996). I expect that Chris Weedon will shortly be added to this list as she too is emerging as one of the few British feminist critics who gets fairly regular mention in American-produced texts. France is the other national location that appears on the list, situated in terms of the numerical hierarchy between the United States and Britain. What became known in the 1980s as 'French feminism' is represented by three women, Hélène Cixous, Julia Kristeva and Luce Irigaray, and laudable attempts to give a wider representation of French feminist thought have never fundamentally dislodged this holy trinity.[4] It is strange that none of these representatives of 'Frenchness' was actually born in France – strange, that is, if nationality of birth retains any meaning: Cixous was born an Algerian Jew, though with French nationality, and of Spanish and German parentage; Kristeva is Bulgarian by birth, Irigaray is a French national but born in Belgium. Not only does French feminism get reduced to three names, but it is also often presented as a synonym for *l'écriture féminine* – certainly the relevant and influential essays of Jones and Showalter make that connection – and then by a process of false deduction the chosen three are indiscriminately interpreted as practitioners of *l'écriture féminine*.

The opposition of 'Anglo-American' and 'French', an organizing principle in a good number of the essays and texts included on the list of introductory collections and readers, is an example of a conceptual debate in feminism constructed in geographical terms. It could just as easily have been constructed in historical terms: feminism influenced by late 1960s and early 1970s radical politics against feminism influenced by the late 1970s and 1980s influx of Continental theory. In either case the opposition has come to be unhelpfully over-simplified, 'that fatal unclutteredness', though not without its interesting ironies. Certainly I am not the only editor/author from that list to exhibit skills in double-thinking, respectfully quoting the piece from Cixous's 'Sorties' where she talks about the deconstruction of patriarchal binary thought, only then to set up in an ensuing commentary two great antagonistic monoliths: the French apparently were like 'this' and the Anglo-Americans were definitely like 'that'. Again a combination of detailed literary history and an analysis of the signification of terms could open this opposition to a necessary deconstruction and could remind us that critical debate does not free-float somewhere in the ether but is grounded in institutions and material practices.

One area of research would be in tracing the import of French feminist thought into the British and American academies: the availability of translations, the publishing of primary and secondary texts, the response in journals, the subject matter of conferences, the work of French departments in Britain and the United States and the research of individual academics 'in' French, the cross-Channel and trans-Atlantic dialogues and networks, the relation between French feminism and other forms of Continental thought – all these aspects need much fuller scrutiny. Some excellent bibliographies are now being published which greatly help our understanding of precisely what became available when, to which audience, amidst what kind of critical arguments. I am thinking of Margaret Whitford (ed.), *The Irigaray Reader* (1991), Susan Sellers (ed.), *The Hélène Cixous Reader* (1994) and Kelly Oliver, *Reading Kristeva: Unraveling the Double-bind*. We can also appreciate the significance of certain texts and journals in setting the debate. 1980 saw the publication of Hester Eisenstein's and Alice Jardine's *The Future of Difference*, which included Domna Stanton's 'Language and revolution: the Franco-American dis-connection'. The same year produced probably the most influential attempt at *connection* in Elaine Marks and Isabelle de Courtivron (eds), *New French Feminisms: An Anthology*. The years 1981 and 1982 proved to be a pivotal period for translations and discussions of French feminism within American journals: *Yale French Studies* (62) printed Spivak's essay on 'French feminism in an international frame'; *Feminist Studies* (Vol. 7, No. 2) published Ann Rosalind Jones's 'Writing the body: toward an understanding of *l'écriture féminine*' and essays by Hélène Vivienne Wenzel and Carolyn Burke on Monique Wittig and Luce Irigaray respectively; *Signs* (Vol. 7, No. 1) contained translations of and introductions to Kristeva's 'Women's time', Cixous's 'Castration or decapitation?', 'Absent from history' and 'The twilight of the goddesses, or the intellectual crisis of French feminism'. *Signs* had already published in 1976 a translation of Cixous's 'The laugh of the Medusa'. Summer 1982 saw the 'Cherchez la femme' edition of *Diacritics* with Elizabeth Berg's review of the work of Sarah Kofman and Luce Irigaray. Amongst British journals it was *Screen* and *m/f* which were most open to a dialogue with France, and in the area of full-length studies the work of Toril Moi – *Sexual/Textual Politics* (1985); *The Kristeva Reader* (1986) and *French Feminist Thought: A Reader* (1987) – determined the debate and the teaching context in a marked way.

Cixous has warned how oppositions are invariably hierarchical though, in the tussle between Anglo-American and French, the dominant term changes according to the critical and political position of the subject. Thus one narrative tells us that the French are fiercely intellectual: look at all those illustrious names and don't they even have philosophical discussions on prime-time television? Sharp, theoretically sophisticated, way beyond the old snares of realism and humanism. In contrast, the Anglo-Americans, poor dears, are naïve, untheoretical, bewildered by the postmodernist world, tied to a plodding pragmatism. The French have glamour and style, all that dazzling word play; the Anglo-Americans still think authors are real people. Reverse the perspective and the story is different. The French are abstract, élitist, speaking only to an audience of polymaths (how many of us know enough about philosophy, linguistics, psychoanalysis, to cope with these texts?); perversely obscure (all those authors you've never read, half of them you've never even heard of); wildly utopian and ahistorical; so agonizingly self-referential that nothing ever seems clearly to get said. The Anglo-Americans, on the other hand, are politically and materially aware, with a strong sense of history and a desire to maintain the link between the academic and the activist. From both sides there are accusations of essentialism: against the French for their idealization of the feminine; against the Anglo-Americans for their attachment to a fixed, knowable female subject. As Rachel Bowlby wittily remarks:

> The party is over, and those people we met on the ferry who turned out to be not our sort after all, have thankfully gone home without breaking too many glasses. Logically, it's time to put the kettle on and decide that we never liked them much in the first place, and also they were wrong, and even if they're right it's not what we need.
>
> (Bowlby, 1992: 118)

Cultural and intellectual differences, deserving of a close and subtle exploration, slide with alarming ease into national stereotypes.

In the earlier collections of essays on the introductory list, geography links with issues of race and ethnicity either in the person of the Afra-American writer and critic or, as we have seen, in the person of Spivak as the singular voice of the Third World. In later volumes (Warhol and Price Herndl, 1991; Humm, 1994; Eagleton, 1996) the understanding of what constitutes the Third World is, in one respect, broadened: Warhol and Price Herndl include material from and about Native American, Chicana and Asian-American feminisms; Humm mentions Indian, Latin American, Aboriginal, Chicana, Chinese-American; I include Indian, Vietnamese, Chicana. Yet, in another respect, the debate that reaches Europe continues to be filtered predominantly through the educational and publishing institutions of the United States. One need look only at the institutional homes of this new group of 'stars': Shirley Geok-lin Lim, University of California, Santa Barbara; Rey Chow, University of Minnesota; Chandra Talpade Mohanty, Oberlin College; Trinh T. Minh-ha, San Francisco State University. Humm has also tried to extend the category 'black' beyond the almost exclusive concentration on Afra-American feminism in earlier collections to include African feminism, Caribbean feminism but, curiously, not black British.

As yet absent from the collections but, I anticipate, a category that will emerge shortly is that of European literary feminism. Hitherto, 'Europe' has had a bifurcated role as the 'Anglo' element attached to 'American' and the 'French' category in opposition to Anglo-American.[5] A series of readers produced by Blackwell Publishers between 1987 and 1993 defined the known world of feminism as France, Britain, Italy and the United States: Toril Moi (ed.), *French Feminist Thought: A Reader* (1987); Terry Lovell (ed.), *British Feminist Thought: A Reader* (1990); Paolo Bono and Sandra Kemp (eds), *Italian Feminist Thought: A Reader* (1991), and Linda S. Kauffman (ed.), *American Feminist Thought: At*

Century's End (1993). No Spain (though, as we have seen, Spanish-speaking feminisms are increasingly represented under the banners 'American', 'Third World' and 'Third World women in the US'), no Germany, no Northern Europe, no Eastern Europe.[6] Terry Lovell's belief in national difference as 'related to specific historical, political and intellectual contexts' (1990: 3) rather than to country of birth or domicile allows her to claim for 'British' feminist thought, amongst others, Juliet Mitchell (born in New Zealand), Germaine Greer (born in Australia), Cora Kaplan (born in America) and Toril Moi (born in Norway). The establishment of *The European Journal of Women's Studies* and of special European issues from existing journals, the creation of European feminist networks and the work of women's groups within the structures of the EEC, the specifically *literary* feminist potential within organizations such as the European Society for the Study of English or through exchange programmes, all point to new configurations of feminist meanings and activity.[7]

Inclusion and exclusion

When editors from the original list introduce their collections or authors their surveys the problem of selection is invariably to the fore. Knowing full well the marginal position of women under patriarchy, all feminists are keen not to reproduce with respect to other women the unequal relationship of central and peripheral, inclusion and exclusion. Yet, of course, the very act of selection necessitates that a few are chosen but most are not. In a sense, deconstructive debates about specific identities – 'black', 'Third World', 'working class' – often displace rather than address the difficulty, just as arguments about the notion of 'the representative' fail to answer adequately legitimate demands for representation by the excluded. At such moments political issues are rapidly transposed into the metaphysical; problems of power and inequality into discussions on shifting signification. From various wings of feminist thought the demand for inclusion can be heard: liberal feminist claims for equal access and equality of opportunity; utopian, poetic visions of unity and sisterhood; deconstructive ploys to introduce the subordinated term; the recognition of multiplicity and difference; Marxist-feminist challenges to hegemony in the name of the oppressed. The megalomaniacal delusions of David Lodge's Morris Zapp, planning to produce the ultimate totalized version of Jane Austen after which nothing more could be said, have not, by and large, bothered feminism (Lodge, 1978: 44–5). Our inclusive delusions are of a more munificent nature, the wish to have all the girls in the team and the concomitant fear of appearing unsisterly or élitist if one doesn't succeed.

Failure, however, is inevitable. Judith Butler's comments on descriptions of feminist identity can be related to our present concern with the writing of a feminist literary history:

> The theories of feminist identity that elaborate predicates of color, sexuality, ethnicity, class, and able-bodiedness invariably close with an embarrassed 'etc.' at the end of the list. Through this horizontal trajectory of adjectives, these positions strive to encompass a situated subject, but invariably fail to be complete. This failure, however, is instructive: what political impetus is to be derived from the exasperated 'etc.' that so often occurs at the end of such lines? This is a sign of exhaustion as well as of the illimitable process of signification itself. It is the *supplément*, the excess that necessarily accompanies any effort to posit identity once and for all.
>
> (Butler, 1990: 143)

Butler illustrates how the aim to be inclusive leads to incomplete lists of oppressed categories, the incompleteness indicated by the inevitable 'etc.'. This 'etc.' Butler sees in a series of ways, both negative and positive – as a sign of embarrassment, exasperation, exhaustion, but also as a sign of the endless process of signification and, in Derridean terms, as an illustration of the *supplément*. Jonathan Culler's gloss is helpful here; he explains Derrida's logic of supplementarity as follows:

> The supplement is an inessential extra, added to something complete in itself, but the supplement is added in order to complete, to compensate for a lack in what was supposed to be complete in itself. These two different meanings of supplement are linked in a powerful logic, and in both meanings the supplement is presented as exterior, foreign to the 'essential' nature of that to which it is added or in which it is substituted.
>
> (Culler, 1989: 103)

What has been traditionally offered as a dominant literary history has in recent years been augmented by new chapters – the history of women's writing or black writing – as Butler says, 'etc.'. These new histories expose the lack and inadequacies of the earlier account but they, in turn, prove inadequate, fuelling demands for histories of, specifically, black *women's* writing or lesbian writing – again, as Butler says, 'etc.'. One ends – except, of course, the process never ends – with a chain of supplements without any original source or any termination; there's no alpha or omega. If one went back to what I termed the 'traditional' history, one would find this too contested and unresolved; if one thought forward to the construction of further narratives, one would always find yet more omissions, more unrepresented or under-represented voices, more 'etcs.'.

Thus the hope for an ultimate volume, *pace* Morris Zapp, is not merely a practical impossibility – at its most basic, the absence of sufficient pages to fit everything in – it is also, in Derridean terms, a philosophical impossibility. As Culler says, 'there is always a lack in what is supplemented, an originary lack' (1989: 103). Even Zapp discovers this at some incoherent level. The 'utterly exhaustive' list of critical positions he proposes reads, Polonius-like: 'historical, biographical, rhetorical, mythical, Freudian, Jungian, existentialist, Marxist, structuralist, Christian-allegorical, ethical, exponential, linguistic, phenomenological, archetypal, you name it' (Lodge, 1978: 44). Significantly, feminism does not feature on the 'utterly exhaustive' list of 1978 and is lost somewhere in 'you name it' as Zapp's, and Lodge's, equivalent of Butler's 'etc.'. To see the writing of women's literary history as a problem of supplementarity might explain our continuing dissatisfaction with whatever we produce and also some of the guilt-ridden tensions which surface within feminism. Not only is any account incomplete, paradoxically full of lack but, as Culler says, 'the supplement is presented as exterior, foreign to the "essential" nature of that to which it is added'; in short, the supplement is regarded as subordinate. This is all too clear in Sandoval's irritation at being relegated to the 'unofficial' story of feminism (1991: 5–6); in Trinh's critique of a token presence as 'A special Third World women issue' (1989: 111); in Rey Chow's complaint about the Chinese woman's location in 'The case study and the culture garden' (1991: 94), or in Shirley Geok-lin Lim's objection to her unwelcome role as 'representative' (1993: 240). In each of these examples, the Third World woman rejects her role as supplement to what is given.

In the selection of material for introductory texts, inclusiveness is sometimes linked to topicality. This is partly a marketing strategy as the book can be billed as 'the most up-to-date introduction to feminist literary criticism' (blurb to Humm, 1994), but it is also an indication of feminism's desire to remain open to new inputs and to resist becoming a canonical closed shop. In particular, in the collections of essays where the number of critics is limited to ten or twelve, inclusiveness gives way to an emphasis on first, 'the representative' and second, 'the relevant', two further minefields in terms of issues about selection. Even where the focus is on a particular mode of feminist criticism, plurality is often stressed: no one wants to be seen as presenting a dogmatic party line. But plurality cannot become randomness and an equal emphasis will be given to finding some kind of unifying pattern. The Introduction of Robyn Warhol and Diane Price Herndl's *Feminisms: An Anthology of Literary Theory and Criticism* (1991) interestingly circulates around all these knotty problems. With its 1118 pages it is by far the largest collection to date and, in its reference to Sandra Gilbert and Susan Gubar's *Norton Anthology of Literature by Women* (1985), suggests that we might read the text as the critical companion to Gilbert and Gubar's collection of imaginative writing. Aiming for 'coherence within diversity' (1991: xiv), it has limited itself to essays relating to nineteenth- and twentieth-century British and North American texts but has also included some French authors 'who have particularly influenced the American critical scene'; that is, the 'relevance' argument. The collection is a 'wide-angle view' (p. x) and a 'wide-ranging picture' (p. xiii) but also the product of certain 'principles' of selection (p. x); it does not offer a 'totalizing definition of feminist criticism', rather it aims to present 'various feminisms' and 'a significant number of voices' (p. xiii); it wants to include 'as many as possible of those statements within feminist criticism that have been repeatedly cited' but also 'to print interesting essays that represent as many current approaches as possible, regardless of the writers' institutional prominence or fame' (ibid.); it acknowledges the restraint of space on its own selection and suggests that an 'ideal collection of feminist criticism' would include at least ten more named organizing concepts and 'many others' (p. xvi). Appropriately the concluding metaphor and the picture on the book cover is of a quilt, a miscellaneous collection of pieces, from a range of contexts, brought together through the skill of women to make an identifiable, harmonious pattern. You can discern even from these short quotations how conscious Warhol and Price Herndl are of the difficulties of selection and how thankless is their task. Naming the problem is not, they implicitly discover, the same as solving the problem and the antitheses they strain to negotiate – diversity versus coherence, space versus confinement, canonical versus non-canonical, open versus selective, free versus controlling – are not capable of resolution. Perhaps we should be stressing in our introductory surveys that what we offer is not 'representative' but over-determined.[8]

When Judith Butler talks of the *supplément*, of the excess which escapes any attempt to fix identity, she sees there a potential both for the human (in our case, feminist) subject and for political change. Her study concludes:

> If identities were no longer fixed as the premises of a political syllogism, and politics no longer understood as a set of practices derived from the alleged interests that belong to a set of ready-made subjects, a new configuration of politics would surely emerge from the ruins of the old.
>
> (Butler, 1990: 149)

My answer to that claim would be yes, I suppose it would; *something* would emerge – but how, through what material and institutional interventions and with what surety that the new configuration would be any more progressive than the old? The 'horizontal trajectory of adjectives' that Butler speaks of may not be able 'to encompass a situated subject', but it has its uses in exposing inequalities of power: one trajectory, say, 'black, female, lesbian, working class, unemployed' is obviously not equivalent to another trajectory, say, 'white, male, heterosexual, middle class, professional'. Butler detects 'embarrassment' in the feminist failure 'to encompass a situated subject' but, then, rather swiftly and briskly, moves the reader on through 'exasperation' and 'exhaustion' to the welcome liberation of the 'illimitable process of signification'.

I notice another rapid movement away from embarrassment in a section from Jane Gallop. Discussing Deborah McDowell's criticism that white middle-class feminists excluded the work of black women from anthologies and critical studies, Gallop responds:

> In the highly moralized context of feminist criticism, it is devastating to discover that white feminists 'perpetrated' the same sort of exclusions as the male critics against whom we are protesting. Yet, following the logic of Zimmerman's investigation of the problem of definition for lesbian critics, we might want to consider this perpetration of exclusion not so much as an ethical failing but rather as the effect of a certain structure, the recurrent tendency in the establishment of a subfield to generate exclusionary definitions.[9]
>
> (Gallop, 1992: 31)

Gallop isn't happy to see feminist criticism as part of a 'highly moralized context'. With one leap she rises above any feeling of the 'devastating' and transforms exclusion as 'an ethical failing' into the less threatening and less charged interpretation of exclusion as a structural problem. Butler's rejection of the fantasy of full subjecthood and her aspiration towards an equally mythic world of diverse and proliferating subjectivities and positions does not answer the present needs, here and now, of subjects excluded from political and cultural representation. The retreats from embarrassment by Butler and from ethics by Gallop strike me as similar strategies of avoidance – avoidance of the legitimate and insistent demands of under-represented groups and avoidance of a sense of personal responsibilities. Butler and Gallop can look to their own consciences; let me look to mine.

My ineptitude in totalizing the subjectivity of the average white middle-class male does not greatly trouble me; my inability to represent with any degree of adequacy the perspectives of many feminist positions does. This is not an inconsistency in my thinking; rather it is a recognition of power differentials and the part I play in them. White middle-class males already have more than their fair share of access to cultural representation and don't need my help. What I cannot so easily accommodate is the fact that my personal trajectory as feminist, white, professional, member of an academic institution, is predicated, in whatever measure, on the absence of other feminists. I gain access at the expense of their exclusion and knowing that inclusiveness is a fantasy doesn't make the privilege any more acceptable. I do not want to circumvent the awkwardness and embarrassment of that situation; I do not want to underplay the ethical responsibilities of it. On the contrary I think relatively privileged feminists have to hold on to a sense of embarrassment and of ethics, not as a self-lacerating indulgence but as a necessary spur to political action. What are the implications of all this for my redrafting of the introductory lecture, 'Who's Who and Where's Where: Constructing Feminist Literary Studies'?

Notes

Mary Eagleton is Senior Lecturer in English and Women's Studies at the University College of Ripon and York St John. This article is the product of an increasing unease about her own critical work which has been concerned largely with the kind of introductions to literary studies which she discusses here: *Feminist Literary Theory: A Reader* (1986; second edn. 1996, Oxford: Blackwell); *Feminist Literary Criticism* (1991, London: Longman); *Working With Feminist Criticism* (1996, Oxford: Blackwell). She is very committed to teaching and to explaining to students the history and importance of feminist literary studies, and wants to find a method of teaching that does not endlessly reproduce all the old hierarchies.

1 On the literary history and critical reception of *The Second Sex* see, for instance, Dietz (1992) and Moi (1994), chapter 7.

2 It is difficult to classify these texts too precisely: some would see themselves as 'surveys'; some as 'introductions'; some as 'collections of key essays'. Moreover, though the emphasis is on literary *theory*, some contributions are also concerned with critical *practice*. The common denominator is the frequency of their use on feminist courses. I have mentioned my own work here as unfortunately there seems no valid case for excluding myself from public scrutiny. I have, however, included only the second edition of my *Feminist Literary Theory: A Reader* (1996) since nearly all extracts from the first edition are included in it and to survey both editions *and* my Longman volume would weigh the selection too much towards my preferences.

3 Some details on how I have quantified this data. In the collections of essays and extracts I have simply noted the names of the authors included. Though popular critics, most obviously Showalter, occasionally feature more than once in a single collection I have counted only one entry. Second, in the case of the literary surveys (Moi and Humm) which mention in passing large numbers of critics, I have counted only those named on the 'Contents' pages as the critics

who are receiving most prominent coverage in the book. Third, there is a clear difference of emphasis between featuring as one of ten selected essays in a collection and as one of a hundred or so extracts and this difference is not represented in the data. However, taking all these factors into account, I doubt if a different calculation of the figures would produce any significantly different results. What I do regret, though, is how concentrating on the oft-repeated names, even if it is to question their pre-eminence, hides, yet again, the less well-known names which are mentioned particularly in Humm and Eagleton (1996). The problem of inclusion and exclusion is one of the issues of this essay.

4 *Feminist Review* gave space in early issues to the materialist feminism of Christine Delphy. See also Delphy (1984), though this study does not consider cultural and aesthetic issues; Duchen (1987) and Moi (1987) both cover a wider spread.

5 The term 'Anglo-American' deserves as much analysis as the term 'French' and, certainly, the distinctiveness of each element in that compound would need examination. See the forum on 'Is There an Anglo-American Feminist Criticism?' in *Tulsa Studies in Women's Literature* 12: 2.

6 The designation 'Third World women in the U.S.' is from Trinh (1989: 99).

7 See, for instance, *Feminist Review* 39 (Autumn, 1991), 'Shifting territories: feminism and Europe'; Braidotti, 1994. Note also the developing interest in feminisms from Australia and the Pacific rim, for example, in the forthcoming publication of *Australian Feminist Studies* (Carfax Publishing Co, 1996).

8 Though I find Warhol and Price Herndl's Introduction excessively dextrous and controlling in trying to resolve all contradictions, it is only fair to point out that the collection concludes with a section entitled 'Alternative arrangements for *feminisms*' which in a more open and creative way suggests permutating the contents to produce varied groupings and juxtapositions.

9 Note: 'perpetrated' is Gallop's quote from McDowell.

References

As bibliographical details of the texts surveyed have been included in the body of the essay I have not repeated the information here. In respect of essays that have been frequently anthologized, I give the original location and a single, easily available anthology reference; the table included in the essay (pp. 7–8) indicates other likely sources.

BEAUVOIR, Simone de (1972) *The Second Sex* Harmondsworth, Middlesex: Penguin.
BONO, Paola and KEMP, Sandra (1991) editors, *Italian Feminist Thought: A Reader* Oxford: Blackwell.

BOWLBY, Rachel (1992) *Still Crazy After All These Years: Women, Writing and Psychoanalysis* London: Routledge.
BRAIDOTTI, Rosi (1994) 'United States of Europe or United Colors of Benetton?' in *Nomadic Subjects: Embodiment and Sexual Difference in Contemporary Feminist Thought* New York: Columbia University Press.
BUTLER, Judith (1990) *Gender Trouble: Feminism and the Subversion of Identity* London: Routledge.
CHOW, Rey (1991) 'Violence in the other country: China as crisis, spectacle, and woman' in Chandra Talpade Mohanty, Ann Russo, Lourdes Torres, editors, *Third World Women and the Politics of Feminism* Bloomington and Indianapolis: Indiana University Press.
CIXOUS, Hélène (1976) 'The laugh of the Medusa', *Signs: Journal of Women in Culture and Society* 1(4), anthologized in **Warhol** and **Price Herndl** (1991).
—— (1986) 'Sorties: out and out: attacks/ways out/forays', *The Newly Born Woman* (trans. Betsy Wing) Manchester: Manchester University Press. Anthologized in **Belsey** and **Moore** (1989).
CULLER, Jonathan (1989) *On Deconstruction: Theory and Criticism after Structuralism* London: Routledge.
DELPHY, Christine (1984) *Close to Home: A Materialist Analysis of Women's Oppression* London: Hutchinson.
DERRIDA, Jacques (1976) *Of Grammatology* (trans. Gayatri Chakravorty Spivak) Baltimore and London: The Johns Hopkins University Press.
DIETZ, Mary G. (1992) 'Introduction: debating Simone de Beauvoir' in *Signs: Journal of Women in Culture and Society* 18(1).
DUCHEN, Claire (1987) editor, *French Connections: Voices from the Women's Movement in France* London: Hutchinson.
EISENSTEIN, Hester and JARDINE, Alice (1980) editors, *The Future of Difference: The Scholar and the Feminist* Boston: G.K. Hall.
ELLMANN, Mary (1979) *Thinking About Women* London: Virago.
FIGES, Eva (1972) *Patriarchal Attitudes* London: Panther.
GILBERT, Sandra M. and GUBAR, Susan (1979) *The Madwoman in the Attic: The Woman Writer and the Nineteenth-Century Literary Imagination* New Haven and London: Yale University Press.
GILBERT, Sandra M. and GUBAR, Susan (1985) editors, *The Norton Anthology of Literature by Women: The Tradition in English* New York: W.W. Norton and Co.
GALLOP, Jane (1992) *Around 1981: Academic Feminist Literary Theory* London: Routledge.
GREER, Germaine (1970) *The Female Eunuch* London: MacGibbon & Kee.
GROSZ, Elizabeth A. (1987) 'Feminist theory and the challenge to knowledges' *Women's Studies International Forum* Vol. 10, No. 5.
JONES, Ann Rosalind (1981) 'Writing the body: toward an understanding of *l'écriture féminine*' *Feminist Studies* Vol. 7, No. 2. Anthologized in **Showalter** (1986).
—— (1985) 'Inscribing femininity: French theories of the feminine' in **Greene** and **Kahn**, editors.

KAMUF, Peggy (1982) 'Replacing feminist criticism' *Diacritics* Vol. 12, No. 2. Anthologized in Eagleton (1991).
KAUFFMAN, Linda S. (1993) editor, *American Feminist Thought: At Century's End* Oxford: Blackwell.
KOLODNY, Annette (1980) 'Dancing through the minefield: some observations on the theory, practice, and politics of a feminist literary criticism' *Feminist Studies* Vol. 6. Anthologized in Showalter (1986).
KRISTEVA, Julia (1981) 'Women's time' *Signs: Journal of Women in Culture and Society* Vol. 7, No. 1. Anthologized in Belsey and Moore (1989).
LIM, Shirley Geok-lin (1993) 'Asians in Anglo-American feminism: reciprocity and resistance' in Greene and Kahn, editors, *Changing Subjects: The Making of Feminist Literary Criticism* London: Routledge.
LODGE, David (1977) *Changing Places* Harmondsworth, Middlesex: Penguin.
LOVELL, Terry (1990) editor, *British Feminist Thought: A Reader* Oxford: Blackwell.
MARKS, Elaine and COURTIVRON, Isabelle de (1980) editors, *New French Feminisms: An Anthology* Brighton, Sussex: The Harvester Press.
McDOWELL, Deborah (1980) 'New directions for black feminist criticism' *Black American Literature Forum* Vol. 14. Anthologized in Showalter (1986).
MILLETT, Kate (1977) *Sexual Politics* London: Virago.
MUKHERJEE, Bharati (1994) *The Holder of the World* London: Virago.
MOERS, Ellen (1978) *Literary Women* London: The Women's Press.
MOI, Toril (1986) editor, *The Kristeva Reader* Oxford: Blackwell.
—— (1987) editor, *French Feminist Thought: A Reader* Oxford: Blackwell.
—— (1994) *Simone de Beauvoir: The Making of an Intellectual Woman* Oxford: Blackwell.
OLIVER, Kelly (1993) *Reading Kristeva: Unraveling the Double-bind* Bloomington and Indianapolis: Indiana University Press.
OLSEN, Tillie (1980) *Silences* London: Virago.
RICH, Adrienne (1987) 'Compulsory heterosexuality and lesbian existence' in *Blood, Bread, and Poetry: Selected Prose 1979–1985* London: Virago.
SANDOVAL, Chela (1991) 'U.S. Third World feminism: the theory and method of oppositional consciousness in the postmodern world' *Genders* Vol. 10.
SELLERS, Susan (1994) editor, *The Hélène Cixous Reader* London: Routledge.
SHOWALTER, Elaine (1978) *A Literature of Their Own: British Women Novelists from Brontë to Lessing* London: Virago.
—— (1979) 'Toward a feminist poetics' in Jacobus. Anthologized in Showalter (1986).
—— (1981) 'Feminist criticism in the wilderness' *Critical Inquiry* Vol. 8. Anthologized in Showalter (1986).
SMITH, Barbara (1977) 'Toward a black feminist criticism' *Conditions: Two* Vol. 1, No. 2. Anthologized in Showalter (1986).
SPACKS, Patricia Meyer (1976) *The Female Imagination: A Literary and Psychological Investigation of Women's Writing* London: Allen & Unwin.
SPIVAK, Gayatri Chakravorty (1981) 'French feminism in an international frame' *Yale French Studies* Vol. 62. Anthologized in Eagleton (1991).

—— (1985) 'Three women's texts and a critique of imperialism' *Critical Inquiry* Vol. 12. Anthologized in Belsey and Moore (1989).
TODD, Janet (1988) *Feminist Literary History: A Defence* Cambridge: Polity Press.
TRINH, T. Minh-ha (1989) *Woman, Native, Other: Writing Postcoloniality and Feminism* Indiana: Indiana University Press.
WHITFORD, Margaret (1991) editor, *The Irigaray Reader* Oxford: Blackwell.
WOOLF, Virginia (1929; 1933; 1993) *A Room of One's Own* and *Three Guineas* (ed. Michèle Barrett) Harmondsworth, Middlesex: Penguin.
ZIMMERMAN, Bonnie (1981) 'What has never been: an overview of lesbian feminist criticism' *Feminist Studies* Vol. 7, No. 3. Anthologized in Showalter (1986).

Situated Voices
'Black Women's Experience' and Social Work

Gail Lewis

Abstract

The article uses a discourse analytic approach to explore some of the ways in which black women social workers invoke the category 'experience' as a means by which to mediate their structural and discursive location in social services departments. The article draws on current feminist theoretical debates about 'experience' and the 'multivocality' of black women as they construct dialogic spaces with diverse interlocutors. In so doing an argument is made for an understanding of 'black women's experience' as constituted rather than descriptive.

Keywords

discourse analysis; black women; social services; 'experience'; contingency

In reconstituting the history of feminism in the post 1960s era, white feminists in Britain and the USA have discussed how consciousness raising groups had the effect of historicizing individual circumstance and experience (see e.g. Wandor, 1990). By sharing the content of everyday life, what was often believed to belong only to the individual was gradually and collectively understood as deeply embedded in a web of social and cultural relations which were themselves rooted in historical change. 'Experience' then was understood as collective and social: 'the personal as political'. This new understanding was to lead to the highly problematic notion of a global sisterhood organized around an appeal to a unified 'woman's identity'. In response, black and Third World (white working-class and lesbian) women protested at this totalizing definition and began to point to differences amongst women. The outcome of these emergent critiques was that the content of 'women's experience' began to be dissembled, which in turn meant that the authority of white middle-class women to construct a singular and hegemonic 'experience' was profoundly challenged (see e.g. Carby, 1982; Parmar, 1982; *Feminist Review*, 1984).

These challenges notwithstanding, the *category* of 'experience' was not rejected by black and other feminists. As a privileged site from which to speak, and so constitute oneself, the category was appropriated for a different content and with an oppositional purpose. As feminist writings by black women on both sides of the Atlantic proliferated (see e.g. Anzaldua and Moraga, 1983; Bryan *et al.*, 1985; Choong *et al.*, 1991; Grewal *et al.*, 1987; Jordan, 1986; Lorde, 1984; Smith, 1983; Sulter, 1990), the constitution of 'black women's experience' was well underway. Embedded within many of these was a notion of claiming a 'voice': a position from which to speak. This 'speaking' was necessary if the specificity of 'black women's experience' was to be articulated and a claim to a self-defined womanhood made. Such a claim had been denied by white feminist texts because of their exclusions and (perhaps unconscious) claims to universality.

At first the category itself remained unchallenged and unproblematized, not least because at this point the explicit turn to post-structuralist theory had not yet exerted its influence on much of black British feminism. Having said this, the endurance of the category is testimony to its tremendous *political* importance and the power of its challenge to dominant epistemologies. For, in creating a legitimacy to speak *from* experience, feminists (black and white) had made it possible to begin to undo established ideas about what it means to 'know'. This, together with the adoption of some post-structuralist insights such as the category of 'the subject', cast new light on and raised new problems about the ways in which social categories and the social/psychic selves which inhabit them are constituted. Those who had erstwhile understood themselves as 'individuals' could now cast new meaning on their lives and think of themselves as historically constituted 'subjects'. They could now become alive to their *gendered* selves. The link to the constitution of a classed 'self' is also apparent in a comment made by Patrick Joyce in his work about class and 'self' in nineteenth-century England:

> In many regards we are still Engels' children, not least the most sophisticated students of the historical formation of subjectivities, [who are] alive to the complexity of textual positioning of subjects, but borne down by the leaden weight of an obsolete view of class *in which 'individual' is the sign of 'middle class', a 'collective self' that of the 'working class'*.
>
> (1994, p. 86, my emphasis)

While the divide between self-knowledge as individual or collective is here a result of class, in the twentieth-century feminist context we can add 'race' as the axis along which this divide is organized. As Nell Painter (1995) has commented, when transposed to the black/white binary, this becomes rewritten as white people having psyches while black people have community. So if white middle-class feminists in the

USA and Britain discovered through a collective process that they are constituted as individual selves and from there celebrate what they deem to be a universal sisterhood, black feminists (people) are denied any such individuality (which the notion of psyche suggests) from which to so 'discover' themselves. Those with an 'always already' 'community' are denied the very element from which such processes of identification are made.

Once the issue of what it means 'to know' is established as a site of contestation, the requisite broadening and deepening of the content of knowledge and experience can be seen as only part of the issue. As a result, if in the early years the sociality of 'experience' began to be accepted, some twenty years or more later, feminists (white and black) in these two national formations (Britain and the USA) have begun to problematize and theorize the category 'experience', to examine its ontological and epistemological status, to see, indeed, how it may be used in politically committed intellectual work.

To do this, some consideration about how to theorize the category of 'experience' is required. Two US-based feminists have turned their attention to this – one white (Joan Scott), the other a woman of colour (Chandra Talpade Mohanty). Beginning with a profound sense of opposition to the foundational status of 'experience' in much academic (and feminist) work, where the category is constituted as 'uncontestable evidence and as an originary point of explanation – as a foundation upon which analysis is based' (1992: 24), Joan Scott argues for a historiography which would reveal the connections between the 'experiences' of different groups, repressive mechanisms and the inner logics by which difference is relationally constituted (p. 25). To get to this, she argues, a problematized notion of 'experience' is required, one in which it is recognized that

> It is not individuals who have experience, but subjects who are constituted through experience. Experience in this definition then becomes not the origin of our explanation, not the authoritative (because seen or felt) evidence that grounds what is known, but rather that which we seek to explain, that about which knowledge is produced. To think about experience in this way is to historicise it as well as to historicise the identities it produces.
>
> (Scott, 1992: 26)

Here, then, the very category of 'experience' itself is established as in need of examination, so that the web of historical relations in which all 'experience' is inscribed is brought to the fore. In this way it is possible to reveal not only the binaries, the boundaries, the closures and erasures which are produced in time and space, but also the subjectivities and identities which it is possible for specific social groups to inhabit in specific places at specific times.

'Experience' is widened, deepened and embedded. While Scott addressed herself to historians and cultural theorists, Mohanty directs her attention principally to white feminists. Writing in a similar vein to Scott, but earlier and with more explicit emphasis on political imperatives (as well as intellectual ones), Mohanty argues that 'experience must be historically interpreted and theorised if it is to become the basis of feminist solidarity and struggle, and it is at this moment that an understanding of the *politics of location* proves crucial' (1992: 88–9, my emphasis).

Inspired by Adrienne Rich's work (1984), Mohanty uses the term location 'to refer to the historical, geographical, cultural, psychic and imaginative boundaries which provide ground for political definition and self-definition' (1992: 74). Her concern with the 'politics of location' is derived from her project (shared with many black feminists) to challenge the singular and unitary notion of 'experience' such that it is at once both constitutive of the individual *and* the collective. Mohanty's criticism of such a formulation of 'experience' is stated thus:

> There seem to be two problems with this definition. First, experience is seen as being immediately accessible, understood and named. The complex relationships between behaviour and its representation are either ignored or made irrelevant; experience is collapsed into discourse and vice versa. Second, since experience has a fundamentally psychological status, [in this approach] questions of history and collectivity are formulated on the level of attitude and intention. . . . If the assumption of the *sameness* of experience is what ties woman (individual) to women (group), regardless of class, race, nation and sexualities, the notion of experience is anchored firmly in the notion of the individual self, a determined and specifiable constituent of European modernity.
>
> (1992: 82, emphasis in original)

Strategically it is key to understand that 'the experience of being woman can create an illusionary unity, for it is not the experience of being woman, but the meanings attached to gender, race, class, and age at various historical moments' (p. 86), that it is important to grasp. Hence the need to 'locate the politics of experience'.

Both Scott and Mohanty suggest that the way to theorize experience is to concentrate on its historical specificity and excavate its embeddedness in webs of social, political and cultural relations which are themselves organized around axes of power and which act to constitute subjectivities and identities. Without such a problematizing of 'experience', the binaries, exclusions and erasures which are embedded in it cannot be deconstructed and thus challenged and transformed.

Part of this task involves an analysis of when and how the category of 'experience' is mobilized. This entails an excavation of the location of specific speakers within multiple systems of subordination – those of class, 'race', gender and indeed sexuality. One writer who has been concerned with explicating the positions black women occupy in multiple and simultaneous systems of oppression is Barbara Smith, the black lesbian feminist literary critic. She emphasized the need to locate the contexts through which fictional texts by black women authors can be read. For her, black women's position could not be understood in a framework which conceived of systems of oppression as either discrete or hierarchical.

> A Black feminist approach to literature that embodies the realisation that the politics of sex as well as the politics of race and class are crucially interlocking factors in the works of Black women writers is an absolute necessity.
> (Smith, 1982: 159)

And as she was to make clear in another, more polemical piece, the systems of class, 'race', gender and indeed sexuality, had to be understood as intersecting and giving rise to a simultaneity of oppression:

> The concept of the simultaneity of oppression is still the crux of a Black feminist understanding of political reality and, I believe, one of the most significant ideological contributions of Black feminist thought.
> (Smith, 1983: xxxii)

More recent work by Mae Gwendolyn Henderson (1992) has adapted Smith's idea of 'simultaneity of oppression' and taken it in new directions. She offers an inspirational approach to the examination of the discourses through which black women constitute their multiple selves, give meaning to the content of their lives and define the parameters within which their 'experience' is produced and lived. As Henderson says, 'black women speak from a multiple and complex social, historical and cultural positionality which, in effect, constitutes black female subjectivity' (Henderson, 1992: 147).

For my purposes the point of interest is the way in which Henderson moves from a recognition of the complex embeddedness of 'black women's experience' to a conception about how black women create a position from which to speak (and write), and the discourses which it is possible to discern in their speech (writing). She begins by suggesting that both 'raced' and gendered perspectives, and the interrelations between them, structure the discourse(s) through which black women speak/write. This she refers to as the 'simultaneity of discourse'.

By using this concept, she argues, it is possible to hold on to the notion of black women as at once 'raced', gendered, classed (and sexual) subjects and thus that they are both '"Other" of the Same, [and] also . . . "other" of the "other(s)"' (Henderson, 1992: 146). The discourses which are simultaneously embedded within, and which serve to structure black women's speech/writing, produce relationships of both difference and identification. This means that black women will speak/write 'racial difference within gender identity and gender difference within racial identity' (p. 145).

While this refers to processes of interaction within and between socially constituted groups in which 'othering' plays a central role, Henderson is attempting to get to another dimension as well. This is the constitution of 'self' that occurs through the simultaneity of discourse. Thus she suggests that the complex multiplicity of black women's positioning results in the discursive production of a 'self' in which 'other(s)' are always present. Black women's selfhood, and the speech/writing through which this is constituted, necessarily contains both a 'generalised "Other" and "otherness" within the self' (p. 146).

Critical examinations of how black women in Britain use the category experience to give meaning to the web of relations in which they are inscribed and of the multivocality which this produces are scarce. This article is based on interviews in which black female social workers talk about 'experience' as a way to make sense of and give meaning to their working lives. It discusses some of their views on the links between 'black women's experience' and social work as a practice; and then considers what conclusions might be drawn about the category 'experience' when 'race' and racism are vectors in the constitution and negotiation of power relations. The article arises out of research I have been undertaking into the formation of 'raced' and gendered subjectivities in specific employment contexts. More specifically, their voices arise in response to two interconnected questions. What, if any, are the particular skills or attributes which black women can bring to social work; and why are these important? There was a high degree of repetition of the major themes around and through which the women constructed their specificity as black women. These themes centred on 'oppression', 'struggle' and 'coming through against the odds', all of which were presented as particular to black womanhood.

'Sisters chant: I struggle therefore I am'

I want to argue that the meanings which these black female social workers constructed about both themselves and their work were produced on similar discursive terrain to that which Henderson identifies in the works of African-American women writers. The processes of identification and differentiation; the implicit use of historical memory; the acute awareness of diverse and subordinate social positionings, are factors which it is possible to trace in the accounts which follow. All of these are located within the context of what might be termed an 'occupational situatedness' which defines the parameters within which the women are speaking. Their construction of 'self' and meaning is, then, cast within (the ever present) shadow of their paid employment and as such they draw on professional discourses in which a 'fit' between 'black women's experience' and the 'nature of social work' is posited.

The accounts are numbered sequentially and at the end of the first extract from a new speaker their 'ethnic origin' is given in brackets.

> 1.a. [GL: OK, and do you think there are any particular skills or qualities that black women can bring to social work?] *(a big nod)* '*I think we have the experience in terms of having to survive, in terms of whether it is limited housing, with our parents growing up, the areas we live in because yes, we can move on after you get into the job situation you know, and the area of schools, we have got all those experiences of having to cope with those problems repeatedly, whether it is going to school or wherever you go to, and having to speak up for yourself, and be heard and be counted, and I think that in social services that's what we are paid to try and empower.*' (African-Caribbean)

Already there are a number of interesting factors being brought into play here. There is the *immediate* invocation of 'experience' as the privileged element defining black women's specificity, but importantly this 'experience' is situated in a social and geographical space where having to cope with a variety of 'problems' is foregrounded. Moreover, the necessity of survival is linked to the creation of a speaking position – a struggle to be recognized – and although she acknowledges that social or occupational mobility in adult life can result in an individual moving away from these circumstances, the early experiences are privileged as being formative and it is these which correspond to the tasks of social work. The purported link between what she sees as black women's experience and the purpose of social work is elaborated and re-emphasized as she continues.

> 1.b. [GL: So you are saying that there is an experience?] '*Yeah, that if you stand up and be counted and speak up for yourself and what you need, and*

don't give up, and I need to keep repeating it, I think that is what you do with a lot of clients you know, with their poor housing or whatever else . . .'
[GL: right]
'. . . you know, you are trying to get them not to just accept things if they are not happy with it, and they feel uncomfortable with it, speak up, and a lot of it is also about the experience of grandparents, so we've experienced a wider idea of family, and the fact that it doesn't damage you. You know some people think that if you don't grow up with your mother and father you are damaged for life, a lot of black people have grown up that way and it hasn't damaged them.'

Apart from the repetition of the themes concerning the empathy with clients which derives from their similarity of experience with black women, the need to 'speak up' and the nature of social work, she also begins to imply a critique of one of the dominant ideas in both psychoanalysis and social work about the place of the biological mother and father in the development of the 'healthy child'. This in turn prefaces a challenge to the pathologization of Caribbean family forms in what follows:

1.c. *'So it is a different way of thinking being brought into social services, of what they will teach you at the college and what others at the top, which is white, tend to think and you know, you can actually give those experiences out to people. A lot of clients will come in and say well have you got children or whatever and I say well even if you don't have children, you have been a part of, whether it is your cousins or whoever, you have been a part of them, whether you take the responsibility to take them to school or whatever.'*
[GL: yeah right]
'You have had that experience, but when you look on it, a lot of white people don't, because em, there are white people who deal with the extended families and they strive on that, but there are a lot of them that are so sort of, em, just take responsibility for the immediate one and so not that broader sense of responsibility.'

In this part of the account the speaker is making a claim for a different form of knowledge, thus giving 'black women's experience' an epistemological status born of its location in a specific body of people. Such knowledge can be imparted to clients, thus replaying the idea that part of the function of social work is to 'improve' or strengthen 'needy' or 'deficient' clients. Here she also explicitly racializes 'black women's experience' by foregrounding the opposition to what she purports to be the predominant approach of white people to family relationships and responsibilities. It is also done in such a way that familial experience becomes recoded as an issue of responsibility. In racializing, she also explicitly works with the binary and plays the opposition 'white/black' –

a move highlighted by the exceptions which she invokes. Moreover in the opening sentence of what follows, her sense of a need to be cautious about making too broad generalizations is undermined by the emphasis which her disclaimer gives to her main point.

> 1.d. *'I mean I don't think that is putting black people on a pedestal, but I think it's you know, talking to people irrespective of ages and so on and in terms of caring and sensitivity, again I don't know whether it is because we have cared for so many people, you know whether we know them or not, sort of like, generations gone past, that again we have put out our hands a lot easier than some white people.'*

This part is important because of the move which is made from individual experience of diverse family forms and differential positioning within contemporary socio-economic relations, on the one hand, to an emphasis on a historical location in modes of caring, on the other. This inter-generational location is then used to make the claim that 'we' are more emotionally generous and have a greater propensity to care. The distinction which has been made between caring *for* and caring *about* (see e.g. Dalley, 1988; Grimwood and Popplestone, 1993) is not made here, but her reference to the inter-generational relation to caring and to the notion of strangers or 'non-kin' (whether they are known or not) would suggest that here she is highlighting the 'caring for' aspect. Earlier it is clear that both forms are referenced. What is equally noticeable is her invocation of the historicity of black women's experience, a factor which she emphasizes when asked to expand on the issue of inter-generationality.

> 1.e. [GL: Could you expand a bit more on the second thing that you said though about the generations of caring for lots of people, what do you really mean by that?] *'It's actually in terms of that we are people, who whether we have done it through history, or through books, or whether we have done it through posters, or music or whatever, but we have actually to some degree identified with people who have fought for causes, whatever you want to say, and we have identified, some to a less degree than others, and we have identified this with people who are not living right in front of us now . . . so you are not blanketed into "I can only understand what is happening in 1994 on the 3rd May", you have this other wider bit em, it's difficult to say.'*

Processes of historical discovery, which are also processes of identification, are foregrounded, and this has the effect of reworking 'experience' into a kind of consciousness of connection and positionality. In so doing the sociality of 'experience' is emphasized, but it is also politicized since the sense of historical connection and continuity is actively constituted through the process of excavation and reclamation of those who have struggled for 'causes'. Moreover, this sense of historical connection to 'fighters' is important for social work because knowledge of such genealogical connection helps create a key resource for dealing with the stresses associated with the job. Hence:

> 1.f. [GL: Why is that important for social work?] *'Social work is a very stressful job and if you don't have that capacity to sort of, em, for that sort of tension, because the tension builds up, and you can relieve it because you have different ways of drawing in on things, you know, and if you don't have that then you will burn out and it will get to you quite quickly and you need that capacity to come into work not say "oh I'm going home and never coming back". It's like hard to say, it's like you can think of a lot of things, but like . . .'*
>
> [GL: No I understand, but is it something particular to black women then these two things that you describe?] *'In terms of my involvement with working with people, whether it is FSU (Family Service Unit), in social work or whatever, in terms of how people react to situations, how they cope with stressful situations, maybe going out to a client who is shouting off, threatening or whatever else, in terms of coping with these things, I see a difference you know, in the way people come back* (to the office) *and it's with them for life. I'm not saying you shouldn't be concerned about your personal safety, but that you have to be able to deal with it, and put it in some kind of perspective, otherwise em, then you just see those people sticking to one thing, and only happy dealing with people they have met before you know, and you can actually see that happening even in terms of new workers coming in and welcoming and that sort of thing. Again maybe it is because a lot of black people have had to go in situations where they have been the only one, sometimes they can welcome people on the other side like going in and with the white workers, say if I am on a course, and the majority of the time I am the only black manager, we haven't got that many anyway, and you will be there, and you will have to talk to them first. If I go on a course with the majority of black people, or a meeting and a few white people come in, then we make them welcome, and it is the same in teams, that sort of thing, students come in, whoever they are, it is that and that sort of ease will help you with clients.'*

There are a number of interesting moves made in this sequence. The first is the way in which she accords to black people a general level of ease with and civility towards white people, even while she constructs a firm boundary between black/white in her use of the words 'people on the other side'. The divide between black and white is also sharply made in her inference to the invisibility of black people to white people, compared to the visibility of white to black. Such invisibility/visibility can be read as both reflective and constitutive of the organization of social relations along axes of 'race' in which 'black women's experience' is partially embedded. Her talk of visibility is also organized around a notion of 'minority' which, though referred to in numerical terms in the examples she cites, is also predicated on an implicit conception of 'minority' as a social position ascribed by some marker of differentiation. To see this more clearly we have to read between the lines in sections of the account. Thus if white people find themselves in a situation where they are a numerical minority they will be welcomed by black people. In contrast, because black people will often find themselves in the minority position they will have an aptitude for dealing with difficult situations which is 'with them for life'. Her use of the ungendered term 'black people' is also notable given that she is responding to the question about black *women*, but as Brooks-Higginbothom (1992) has pointed out, 'race'-talk often acts as a metalanguage through which other axes of power, which organize social relations and construct positions, are at once spoken and masked.

The discursive resources she mobilizes to give meaning to various sorts of interactions in which social workers might find themselves are then expanded to suggest that the combined result of 'experience' and historical identification act to produce people with a greater capacity to cope with stressful situations. This differential capacity is exemplified in the ability to place potentially dangerous situations in a wider context. Though not stated, the chains of association which are embedded in her account include the potential threat of racial and/or sexual assault which black women always face. That this is so is embedded in the psyches of all black women in Britain, but this does not mean that they are incapacitated by this potential. Understanding of these dangers, together with historical consciousness of the struggles waged by predecessors, not least in anti-slavery and civil rights struggles, means that the range of threats one might encounter in the course of a social workday takes on a different dimension. Herein lies the importance and relevance for social work, because having staff with this capacity has implications for how workloads are managed, stress is dealt with and interpersonal relations organized.

It is clear then, that the idea of a 'black women's experience', rooted in historical and contemporary relations, acts as a powerful discourse through which the benefits to social work are constructed. It shifts away from any simple idea of ethnic matching between client and social worker as being the way to deal with the requirements of operating within multi-ethnic populations. This shift is achieved because she uses her argument to suggest that the strengths which such 'experience' produces in people who have undergone it are impartable to all clients and other staff. Moreover, the characteristics of the clients of social work are such that it is not just black clients who need these skills, but all or most of them. Employing black social workers can thus act as a resource for the whole department and all its clients.

Having said this, the language in which she gives her account accords to 'black women's experience' an ontological status which is in part undermined by her suggestion that its usefulness for work with clients is racially non-specific. For if such an 'experience' is shared across sections of the black community and across generations, one would expect the survival skills, which she says flow from the 'experience', to be present among black clients. This contradiction arises from her focus on the usefulness which Social Services departments can derive from *employing* black women as social workers, and thus she seeks to stress their specificity in these terms. That there is an unproblematized category called 'black women's experience' is the ground on which she makes the claim to specificity, a claim which would be undermined if she had to begin to explore its points of discontinuity among black women. Such constructions and contradictions raise interesting issues which I will return to in the discussion section of this article and in the light of points raised in the opening section; similarly the slip between 'black women' and 'black people'. Because this slippage is a frequent occurrence throughout the numerous accounts, and indeed sometimes in the formulation of my own questions, from now on I will draw attention to it by marking the words 'women' and 'person/people' in bold. I want now to explore whether similar discourses can be found in the accounts of others.

> 2.a. [GL: And do you think there are any particular or special qualities or skills that black women can offer social work, specifically black women?] *'Yeah, em I think . . . I think personally because this authority sets up so much things against black* **women***, I think for a black* **person** *to actually reach the level of being a social worker and attaining qualifications, they have demonstrated already the amount they have to offer, because they have had to fight off so much things you know to start with. But thinking more of myself, yeah, I think I have a lot of understanding of you know, em, oppression and you know, and can, my strongest quality I would say, is being able to enhance people, because I think I had to do that myself, and I just like to sort of do that, I just think we are strong. I think black women are strong and we are fighters and we will work with a particular case, we will ultimately want to do the best for them.'* (African-Caribbean)

> 2.b. [GL: So where does this strength come from that you are talking about?] *'I think it's like, sort of like, fighting everything that is against you, you are fighting the sexism, you're fighting and you know you fight a lot of things within our own community as well, in terms of our male partners or whatever, in terms of parents, or children, or whatever, we do a lot of things on top of,*

our role is not just you know, it is, even from the social worker, outside of work I have so many other hats that I wear you know. I just think it is more like the oppressiveness predominantly from the white society and structures and whatever.'

Apart from a general repetition of the major themes already encountered in the first account, some of the differences in the language used here are interesting. The first thing to note is that the structure of address shifts from the detached, second person singular, 'you', to the first person plural, 'we', and in so doing she begins to construct a community. Again the thread which binds this community centres on the experience of oppression, the multiple sites of those oppressions, and that the experience derives from the structural location of black women/people.

In developing the idea of struggle against institutions and structures, she suggests that black social workers are a physical embodiment of this struggle because they are a concrete example of achievement against the odds. It is at this point that she first makes the slip from 'black women' to 'black people'. In constructing black social workers in this way she introduces the link between 'black women's experience' and social work as an institution in a slightly different way from the first speaker. Thus although she refers to the empathy which this experience produces between client and black female social worker, she adds to this by saying that the SSD is itself a major locus of the oppression that black women/people suffer (*'This authority sets up so much things against black women'*).

Another shift of emphasis from the first speaker is that here there are specific references to issues internal to the ethnic community she cites as her own. It is an example of Henderson's contestatory discourse with a group constructed as 'community' but who stand in an 'ambiguously (non)hegemonic' position in relation to black women. Thus her contestatory discourse points to the issue of gendered power relations between black women and men, and generational power differentials within families. In so doing she constructs a less 'innocent' picture of black family and 'communal' life. This, together with her indication of the temporary nature of the authority and power she may derive from her occupational status (*'even from the social worker, outside of work . . .'*), in turn allows her to point to the shifting and multiple subjectivities and identities which black women inhabit. But if sexism and age-related subordination are referenced as partially determining 'black women's experience', in the end she foregrounds class and racism as the primary modalities structuring that experience.

2.c. [GL: Why is that important for social work though?] *'I think because social work is a role where unfortunately it targets a community that is like, you know under poverty . . . the majority of our clients seem to fit into that category, and I think the understanding of wanting to bring them out of that, or to offer alternatives, I just think it is, em, it is only where we are at, I mean like in this office, I know I am a social worker and everybody knows I am a social worker, but when I walk out, even around this community, nobody really knows until I say or show my identification of whatever . . . I think it is because we are always having to advocate for ourselves, and I think that the role of a social worker is primarily about advocating for our clients. I think it is one of the things we bring to it.'*

Here again we have the exposition of a social proximity to clients, a construction of social work as an occupation of advocacy on the part of those who, because of poverty, are less able to do it for themselves, and in this way she introduces a notion of class. Her reference to the tenuous nature of the role/status of 'social worker' contrasted to the enduring subject position of 'black person' is how she introduces racism. This of course points to one of the principal features of societies structured in 'race'; that is, the tenacity and pervasive character of racial ascriptions and identifications. For this woman, it is this which speaks to a 'core' 'self', while a 'self' constituted through an occupation is vulnerable because it is invisible in most situations and contexts. Hence if in some senses black people can be invisible, in others they are never able to be free of this marker of social identification and differentiation. There is thus a paradox highlighted here in that it is the very visibility of the marker which creates the conditions for invisibility.

3.a. [GL: Now I want to ask you a question specifically about black women social workers and I am wondering if you think there are any special qualities, skills or experiences that black women can offer social work?] *'Yes there is a variety of skills and knowledge that we can offer, em, I said the majority of us by nature are survivors, and we know how to survive in society, among all the things that we have to face, racism, sexism, disability, whatever it is em . . . em, we feel, I feel when I look at the way we operate with our case list, we tend to be more logical, and we tend to organize ourselves that much better, and we have a high turnout in our cases, and we don't hold on to them for the sake of holding on to them. As soon as they need closing we just close them and get rid of them.'*
[GL: This is black women you are talking about?] *'Yes, most of the black women social workers that I work with'* [GL: And by black women now, do we mean African-Caribbean or do we mean all?] *'African-Caribbean that I have worked with and what I have seen and what I have worked with during my placements and things like that.'* (African-Caribbean)

This speaker gives a clear and unhesitant affirmation that black women have something special to offer and again this is said to be rooted in the strengths which are deemed to derive from experience of, and resistance to, the oppressive matrix of social relations organized around a variety of axes. This is understood to give rise to a positive approach to work organization and 'getting the job done'. There is also an interesting 'naturalization' of the purported survival skills of African-Caribbean women. In the following passage, she focuses on the office hierarchies and their associated job demarcations and responsibilities and the ways in which black women's 'naturally' confident and methodical approach to the work disorganizes these hierarchies and demarcations.

> 3.b. *'We tend to, the managers say to us "I'm the manager I should have made that decision" and . . . we tend to have to, if you are going along doing our cases we plan it, I mean like most other social workers I guess, you know as well you have to plan your case, it's what you are doing anyway, but whereas we will go and start making whatever we need to do to achieve our goals, em, managers, when we come back and sit down in supervision, we'll be told "well you should have discussed that with us". Maybe it is not unique to us but that is the experience that we have had.'*

In addition to the points already mentioned, what is notable about this passage is the shift between the impersonal 'you' and the communal 'we' when she wants to emphasize the specificity of black women's approach to the work. She marks the boundaries between black women and other social workers in this way and the meanings she attaches to managerial responses in supervision are constructed through the prism of 'race'. Later her constitution of a racially and sexually bounded community is crystallized.

> 3.c. [GL: When you say through our experiences, what sorts of things do you mean?] *'Through growing up, especially, like say, the way we had to grow up in the system. . . . Going into the education system and things like that and the issues that you face in your own home life as well . . .'* [GL: What sort of things in your own home life?] *'The way you are expected to be a **black person**, and the stereotyping of how a **woman** should behave, and to be challenging that, like quite a few black **workers**, they feel they are going out of their station to be going into the white man's world and be working and . . .'* [GL: By whom are they seen?] *'By our own, black people. Or you are getting too independent, women are supposed to be here doing this, doing that. . . .'*

This reference to the fracturing of the African-Caribbean population along axes of gendered power relations disrupts any idea of a harmonious and homogenous community, and her intimation that black personhood and black womanhood are constructions is notable because it is the first time that such a suggestion is made in this way. In effect she adopts a multivocality and thus suggests that 'black people' are produced in tension and opposition to 'white people'; 'black women' are produced in tension and opposition to 'black men'; 'black workers' in tension and opposition to 'white managers/power'. This last point moves the passage on to a slightly different register. She restates a link commonly made by black people between power and white males, with the effect that the gendered nature of social work as a *profession* is submerged under a gendered discourse of *power*, and power is conceived as a racialized (not gendered) field (of coercion). She does this by tapping into discourses which construct 'the white **man's** world' as antithetical to black **people's** interests. Thus she assumes I as her black woman interlocutor will be able to read, hence her later reference to 'our own'. To enter 'the white man's world' means to cross over, to not only 'forget' who you are, but also to enter into roles of control over other black people. The result of this is that it creates a barrier to the processes of identification between black social worker and black client. She continues:

> 3.d. '. . . but having to work through those kinds of issues, and then being able to transfer the skills into your work environment and into your caseloads as well, and I guess sometimes . . . sometimes you get frustrated, and you find your mind is rolling ahead, and you are thinking this should be happening, this should be happening, but you tend not to think that the client still has to work through the process, like how you had to work through it, through whatever problem they are going through.'

This is the first time that the control aspects of social work are even hinted at, since whenever 'black women's experience' has been linked to social work it has been to emphasize its caring or enabling side. It is also the first time that the possibility of tensions between black social worker and black client are implied, and the first time the strains that this tension produces for black social workers, as opposed to those between white colleagues, managers or institutions, are suggested.

> 4.a. [GL: OK, let's come back to the issue . . . of why black women staff. . . . You have sometimes referred to the ways in which sometimes it is racism, or conceptions of 'race', but there is gender and perhaps sexuality, all at play. . . . On the other hand, you have talked about . . . black people have something to offer Social Services and I want you to say about what it is they have to offer, whether there is something particular that black women can offer?] '*I mean I would say so, people might disagree with me there, because our experiences are different, we experience different things on the whole, you know, but I would say so, I think as a race, or as races, as well as individuals, but also living in this country having experienced the racism, I think we*

have got a certain amount of resilience, I would say that for most of the social workers do you know what I mean, so you know **there is something extra there**.' (her emphases) (African)

4.b. [GL: But why is that important potentially for Social Services and what is it, you say you are resilient, I want to say to you 'so what'?] *'Erm, well I am thinking now in terms of service users OK, so I am thinking in terms of what we can erm, I was gonna say impart although that's not the right word, but you know, I was gonna say like role models, but no, like being able to support people who have been in, or have experienced, or are experiencing very difficult situations, so on that level.'*
[GL: Yes but why can you support them more than a white woman colleague?] *'I think because their experiences have been different'* (said very quietly).
[GL: So the experience that you say as a black woman you have, gives you something particular? Is it another form of identification? Perhaps with the experiences of black clients, or . . .?] *'Yeah that is along the lines I was thinking, em, I'm just trying to think of an example to make it clearer.'*

4.c. [GL: Yeah, I mean you can talk more generally if you like, it's just that I want you to say a bit more about it, if possible.] *'Well I suppose from my experience of service users, I have worked with a lot of single parents for one, so in terms of their experiences, whatever they might be or whatever their particular situations might be, there are often issues that come up to do with violence, or abuse, or both; to do with black men leaving; em, to do with their position in society, to do with not having power, you know all those sorts of issues, and I suppose I feel because I am a black woman and I have experienced some of those things, and the racism as well, I feel empowered to do certain things and make certain changes and I feel that as black women we can impart something, or we can facilitate some sort of change in service users at that level.'*

4.d. [GL: So it is common experience that forms the basis of this particular stuff that black women can offer?] *'Either common experience, or experience that is similar and I suppose the effects of racism and challenging racism and all that to me is a similar experience, you might not have exactly the same but you might need similar tools to deal with it and you can transfer those tools.'*

The more lengthy interaction between myself and this speaker is noticeable in the ways in which I formulate the questions and it is evident that at times this produced a thoughtfulness or hesitancy in some of her reiterations. However, this hesitancy gave way to firmly articulated views when asked to expand. Again there is a repetition of a language, in which strength, survival, resilience, as products of the experience of racism, is highly profiled. 'Races' are identifiable and bounded communities, but the idea that the term 'black' covers more than one 'race' is implicit in passage 4.a. This 'experience' gives rise to a type of person, but for her this 'person' seems to be one with an *additional* skill or capacity, rather than a person of a completely different 'type' as suggested in some of the other accounts. For example, this speaker's formulation of 'something extra there' is in contrast to the formulation by the third speaker that 'we tend to be more logical'. This 'something extra' acts to demarcate black women from white women.

Similarly the connection to service users is spoken in a similar language to that already heard, although this speaker seems to particularly focus on links to, and empathy with, black service users. This is less clear in other voices. Significantly, in this formulation the changes that social work can effect on clients suggests that they are the objects which are acted upon by a social work subject – to 'facilitate some sort of change in service users'. Experience of and against racism is the privileged factor which can produce this ability, but that this is so does not detract from the echoes of beneficient 'improvement' which was the hallmark of so much nineteenth-century charity and early twentieth-century social work discourse. Moreover, such a discourse has a twentieth-century 'professional' version in the form of viewing social workers as major agents of change (personal, and to some extent social). In this there is a link to the establishment of psychology as the main element in the knowledge base of social work training. Thus, social workers have a key role to play in the rehabilitation of pathologized individuals and families. What is also interesting about this passage is that the speaker herself seems hesitant about using a language which carries these meanings. There is a suggestion in the way in which she formulates her response that she is struggling to find words which are least laden with precisely these nineteenth-century 'charitable' and twentieth-century 'professional' discourses (cf. Rojek *et al.*, 1988).

> 5.a. [GL: Right. Do you think there are any particular or special qualities that black women from diverse communities can offer social work?] 'Qualities?' [GL: Or skills, attributes.] *'Well because either, talking about qualities, I think about understanding and awareness of the immediate culture that they work with it does matter, and language is a skill, and is a special quality. So yes, I do think they are better skills, if utilized and taken into account.'* [GL: Better skills than?] (laughter)*'Better skills than white people working with ethnic minority background people.'* (South Asian)

Here she firmly places the advantage of employing black women social workers in terms of *cultural* understanding and linguistic ability rather than in terms of a historical and contemporary 'experience'. Of course there has been evidence in earlier accounts about knowledge of, and embeddedness in, particular cultural or racial communities, but, as we have seen, in those cases this was superimposed upon racism as the central principle organizing 'black women's experience'. As this speaker continues, her construction of cultural knowledge as ungendered is both emphasized *and* undermined as the issue of gender becomes more complexly posed.

> 5.b. [GL: And are those skills, you know, language, background, familiarity with culture, etc., the things you described, could men from the black communities also offer that?] *'Men!?'* (sharp intake of breath) [GL: Men, black men in other words.] *'Yes, because they can identify themselves, and they understand, not as much as a woman to a woman could, but they would be much more aware of the tradition.'*

Her initial surprise at the idea of thinking about the role of men in this context is clarified when her emphasis on cultural knowledge and understanding as the key modality for good practice in social services is remembered. The way in which she puts the relation is such that she does not speak in absolutely ungendered terms, but rather maps a gendered differential on to a white/non-white binary. And it is this latter one which is fundamental. Once this is established, it is possible for her to elaborate on the ways in which gender enters to structure the relationship between social services and its 'ethnic minority' clients. Thus:

> 5.c. [GL: But is there something absolutely particular to black women from all the diverse black communities, that black women from those communities can offer, even more, or over and above that offered by men from those communities?] (pause). *'Oh, I don't think so, because in this profession one has to be supportive and sympathetic, but I mean the majority of our clients are women anyway. And I feel they feel comfortable with a female, rather than a male.'* [GL: Why?] *'Well I can speak for the South Asian women, find it much easier to talk about personal issues to a female rather than a man, certain things could be affecting them but they can't come out and that is why I think, yes, a woman would be more approachable than a man. I worked with a social work assistant who was a South Asian male, and my clients still faced a problem, allowing him in the house, they wouldn't want a man to knock on the door and come in and if it was a woman it would have been easier for both. Personally, in my role, I did have a problem in seeing myself as a certain member of a respected community, if I had to go along with my colleague, and it wouldn't be as nice as it would be if I went on my own or with a female colleague. There is a certain reputation about women working in a profession, and then working with male colleagues, and the reception of the community would be different.'*

This extract is interesting because of the way in which her opening denial of any gendered specificity immediately moves on to argue the opposite. Her initial denial is premised on a notion of the caring nature of the profession. This means that all social workers must be able to sympathize, if not empathize, with any client. It is, as it were, a professional requirement. But when her focus shifts from the profession to the client base of social work, gender can then enter the field. In contrast to earlier speakers who focused on 'raced' experience (and sometimes class) as the basis of a connection between social worker and client, this speaker highlights gender itself. Similarly, while the gender identification must be underwritten by a cultural sameness and understanding, her differentiation between South Asian male and South Asian female social workers tends towards a primacy of gender. Moreover, gender acts to structure her own 'experience' of the *work*. This in turn is linked to cultural views about the world of professional labour and its purported erosion of gender boundaries operating within specific ethnic communities. So here we have some substance given to the suggestion made by other speakers that part of the issue for women from black communities is the hegemonic prescriptions about how a woman from 'their community' should behave. Because the starting point for this speaker was an emphasis on culture, the *intra-communal* dynamics affecting the social worker/client interaction is foregrounded, whereas for earlier speakers the emphasis on combating systems of racist oppression meant a focus on the *inter-communal* dynamics structuring the relationship. Her own status is spoken of in similar terms, such that her positioning within both the professional institution and 'the community' is constructed in relation to the tension between them. Again it is not that an awareness of the affects of an interstitial positioning has not been mentioned before, but the profound emphasis on something called 'black women's experience' is absent from this account. It is hard to offer any convincing explanation of this difference. Certainly one can raise the question about a possible link to the differential racializations between people of African-Caribbean and South Asian origin descent; for example, the organization of racism directed at South Asian populations in Britain around *cultural* 'othering'. However, the very small numbers of women of South Asian origin/descent in the sample make any more authoritative suggestions inappropriate. The value in pointing to the difference here is twofold. On the one hand, the difference serves to shed light on the dominant discursive repertoires in the accounts. On the other hand, presentation of an alternative way of constructing the specificity of black women's potential contributions to social work shows what terrain is opened up when the category of 'experience' is foregrounded as the vector through which meaning is constructed.

Boundaries of 'race': boundaries of gender

Processes by which 'communities' are discursively produced necessarily involve processes of differentiation and exclusion. Recourse to some essentialized characteristic(s) (biological, social, even material) is made in order to construct the foundational elements of the 'us' as against 'them'. In the preceding section that foundational element in the constitution of the 'community of black women' was 'experience'. 'Experience' was seen as giving rise to an internal strength, an ability to empathize with clients, a methodical and unhesitant approach to the work. This was constructed as rooted in historical as much as contemporary social relations, but a key marker was oppression (always racism, but sometimes also oppression deriving from other axes of differentiation and power) and resistance to it. In short, each account gave rise to a harmony of voices in which it was proclaimed that being a black female social worker was being a particular 'type' of person. A number of issues arise from this which I will consider below. However, I will first briefly consider the ways in which the boundaries of the 'black women's community' were in part established in terms of the limits or connections to white women and black men.

'Us' and white women

> 6.a. [GL: But two things I want to ask you, one is that you have talked about how outside of the office situation black women wear lots of hats and do a lot of things in their role as women outside, but doesn't that apply to white women?] *'It does to an extent, but just because of racism, it clouds everything, every area, so it can't be, I just don't think it can be as bad, there is no way it can be as bad, it can be similar to an extent but I think racism tips the scales you know.'* (African-Caribbean)

Similarly:

> 7.a. [GL: OK, and what about white women can they bring those qualities based on their experiences?] *'Some . . . but not erm, because I think it is different yeah, I just think that their experiences have been* (pause) *yeah, maybe I am talking off the top of my head but I do feel that their experiences have been different, I mean I think they tend to look at things from a different perspective, and even if white women have experienced racism in terms of having a link with black people, I think because of our histories, even just talking about some of these difficult things is going to be difficult and the understanding of it, Oh I can't explain it very well, but yeah* (pause) *I suppose because there is racism in the middle that is going to affect the process.'* (African)

It is notable that this speaker recognizes that racism can also affect white people (white women with black children, which is perhaps the example most often encountered in social work). However, if they can get a proximity to it, they cannot feel or experience it in the same way. The divide which results from being a white or black person erects an indissoluble boundary which determines experience. Thus despite the variation between this speaker and the previous one, the way she poses the situation re-establishes the closeness between them because they both see racism as an essentially black experience. The boundaries created by racialized experiences are clearly expressed in the words of the following speaker.

> 8.a. [GL: Yeah, but you said they (i.e. black women) can bring in real experience, now your white . . . women, don't they have real experience outside?] 'Yes.' [But what are the differences?] *'They bring in real different things, they bring in their real experience as black women, the cultural experience and life experience, which no matter how much you live in England, and no matter how much contact you have with white people – you can live with them, and you can be friends with them, everything – your experience is still different to theirs and that is the bottom line. I mean they have positive real experience, but it is different.'* (African-Caribbean)

So 'black women's experience' is the factor which authorizes the construction of the boundary between black women and white women. Racism is the modality most emphasized as the factor creating differential experience, with some reference to 'culture'. Moreover, the boundaries between the two constituencies are expressed as fixed and immutable – *'you can be friends with them, everything, your experience is still different to theirs and that is the bottom line'*.

Having said this, the fact that these discussions were taking place in the context of a specific occupational setting meant that issues of work informed the ways in which the boundaries were constructed. When pushed further, some of the women began to suggest that the boundaries were perhaps more susceptible to manipulation, at least in the work context, than might be expected from things said earlier.

For example, the following speaker goes on to say:

> 9.a. [GL: Yeah right, so what I'm thinking is then, how do we get beyond, how can you envisage us getting beyond a situation where white social workers can take black cases and do it in a way and not be stumped . . . because if it is about experience, well our experiences in the foreseeable future are going to be quite different . . . yet earlier you were talking about the need for there to be cases allocated on the basis of a number of criteria, not just that you are the same 'race', so how do you match those two things?] *'I suppose it gets down to personalities as well, because I mean even though I say, and I do, that there would be different, you know . . . like one*

service user might get three different people and get different feelings towards them or be able to work in different ways with each of them and I suppose it is not as if to say they are not going to eventually achieve the same goal, but it could be a slower process, it could be a smoother process, those sorts of things. . . . But within that you can have white people, I hope this doesn't sound patronizing, but you . . . could have white women who could work well with a black family and you could have other people who have no experiences and totally, and I think that this is damaging . . . so I am not saying that nobody can, but I think people need to be aware, self-aware as well and if you think this is not appropriate for you then you shouldn't take it on, and in terms of moving forward, I think that if people are looking to work in a particular area, then they need to have some training and some decent training, not just any old thing. I remember when I was in Fostering and Adoption and I went on a training course "Working With West African Families" . . . and it was a white woman running it, and 90 per cent of the people on the course were white, and they left thinking "oh, I can work with West African families", and it was a white woman who did it. I think she had been to Nigeria twice or three times, and spent some time with a family and said "they are so kind because they will even give you their food, even if they haven't got much, they will give it to you" in a very patronizing sort of way, and I'm not talking about that level of awareness and you would be surprised but you still have people operating in that kind of way and I suppose it is about the degree to which people can actually take on board, you know and look at interactions and everything . . . there are two forums just within this office that work could take place, plus we have our central training section and social services training section. So they could have a series of days looking at race and culture and all that sort of stuff. . . . But the thing is, ever since I have been here, I think we have had one debate on race and as it so happened I was the person who had put it on the agenda'. (African)

This long passage makes it clear that the issue of the barriers between black and white women was being constructed within the context of a specific organizational setting where the issues of 'race', racism and culture were thought to be continually marginalized and/or reduced to simplistic and patronizing 'culture tours'. This resulted in the discussion of similarities and differences within gender groups quickly moving into a discussion of the institutional approach to issues of 'race', racism and culture, and the organizational practices which authorize this approach. Experience of a white woman's approach to a specific training issue is used to both exemplify the problem and to justify the argument that black and white women's experiences are so different as to prevent any meaningful fluidity across the boundaries of 'race' and culture. The field of contestation is racism, but it is spoken through a reification of 'race'. This has been evident throughout the accounts where there has been an emphasis on 'struggle', 'fighters', etc. Thus implicit in these sequences is the idea that if racialization and racism did not exist, there would be no need for these terms. The situation with black men is slightly different.

'Us' and black men

Henderson has suggested that black women stand in equivalent distance of difference and identification with white women and black men. Black women's simultaneity of discourse delineates the specifics of the relation to one or the other but addresses both these groups as ambiguously (non) hegemonic. We have already seen from the above extracts that the black women speaking here certainly point to their difference from both white women and black men. However, it is less clear that they draw points of different but equidistant identification between the two. Indeed, with regard to white female social workers, identification was at the very best fragile, even if there was variation in the ways in which speakers constructed the boundaries. Let us now listen to how speakers construct relations with male social workers. It will be seen that the most notable point is that the discursive construction of difference between themselves and black men was less sharply defined for two reasons: first, because the talk was often more embedded in reflections on the general difficulties facing them as *black* female social workers. The following extract was a typical formulation.

> 10.a. *'When I say I am a black woman, I know my black male colleagues find that terrible, if we are talking about racism and I talk about sexism, they say why are you talking about sexism, and I say I am oppressed and you oppress me sometimes, and they can't see it . . . but as a woman as well, I experience sexism, and the power issues when I go into certain schools and talk to head-masters and when I am on the phone, and maybe to some headmasters I am speaking, I might speak received English, you know white English. So they think it is a white person coming in to see them, and when they see you it is like hey "hello"?!. After that they never return calls . . . the one particular headmaster who is working with one of my Asian families, I have been trying to contact that man since December* (six months) *to talk about work we are doing with this particular child, and I have only just managed to get in touch with him. . . . I said the parents are concerned that you said he needs to go to a residential school, and they feel if that is going to happen they want him to go* ('home', i.e. to country of parents' origin). *And he sort of said to me, well the family is the one who said they want him to go . . . and anyway we haven't got the resources* (needed for) *this child . . . I said, well if he does need it, what are you going to do? I personally don't feel he needs it, residential . . . but educational psychological work alongside him . . . and his family. And he goes, no, because there is no consistency with the family home, and whatever work is done in school, would it be followed up, and he thought there were more severe cases in the school. . . . And I*

was so annoyed, I said I will get on to our psychologist and services and I put the phone down, and I spoke to my team manager about it, and . . . I asked him to phone the school, that man, to me, I said to my manager that I cannot prove that it is to do with me being a black woman social worker professional, and he is a white male head teacher . . . and I found it really, really offensive.' (African-Caribbean)

What is notable about this passage is that while she starts off by referring to the points of difference between black female and black male social workers which arise because of the power inequalities associated with gender, she gives far more time and energy in the pace and tenor of her account to the issues which arise from racism and sexism in relation to white men. This is where the reader 'feels' the strength of the obstacles she encounters during the course of her work. Of course, the irony is that the interaction between herself and the headmaster is mediated by another white man (her manager), but this only serves to reinforce the sense embedded in the account that it is in this relation that her gendered 'self' is most acutely felt.

The second reason why boundaries between black women and black men are less sharply delineated arises from the ways in which meanings are conveyed through non-verbal forms of communication, for example, tone, facial expression or other bodily signs. These signs often acted to emphasize the relative strengths or weaknesses of the delineation between themselves and black men in comparison with white women. The reading of these signs was intimately connected to the interaction between two black women: one as interviewer, the other as interviewee. For example:

11.a. [GL: But then I want to ask you, black men suffer racism too . . . they may not have the same kind of gender issues, . . . but they have racism as well. So if the marker between black women and white women is racism, and that is the key issue that makes black women strong, then wouldn't it just make black **people** strong?] *'Yes it does make black people strong, but specifically if we are just going to relate it to white women, I would have to say yeah, that is for me one of the higher dividing things, but yes black men experience racism as well, but I think black women we can experience oppression from our black men even in a professional setting as well as in the home or social settings as well. So it is like in a cocoon and we are just fighting everybody, just to get what we want.'* (African-Caribbean)

Her use of the words '*one of the higher dividing things*' in connection to the boundaries racism constructs between black and white women immediately suggests that the points of tension and distinction between black women and black men will be less emphatically enunciated. So while this speaker consistently raised points about the differentiations between black women and black men, she always suggests a more absolute divide between black and white women. Racism is privileged because *'racism tips the scales you know'*.

Brooks-Higginbothom (1992) has argued that 'race acts as a "global sign" or "metalanguage", since it speaks about and lends meaning to myriad aspects of life that would otherwise fall outside the referential domain of race' (p. 253). Acting as a metalanguage it simultaneously provides a resource against racist subordination, while occluding problems of power internal to black communities around issues of gender, class or sexuality and thereby obstructing their resolution (p. 273). This twofold process is in evidence in extracts 10 and 11 above. The effects of the hegemony of 'race' as a metalanguage are such that these speakers appear less willing or able to construct a harmony of interests within the same gender group, and tend to soften the boundaries of difference between themselves and black men. This does not mean however that they do not mention such a boundary but rather that we need to be cognizant of the contexts which provide the frame within which their accounts are constructed, and listen to the subtexts which are embedded in their speech.

Colouring the category: 'racing' the experience

In their different ways the authors considered at the beginning of this article argued for a reading of 'experience' against the grain of 'common sense'. Rather than taking its ontological status for granted, 'experience' needs to be situated in wider configurations of social, cultural, economic and political relations if the specificities of certain constellations of 'experience' are to be excavated. Only through such a situational reading can the subjectivities and identities produced by 'experience' be understood and analysed. But added to the 'big' locations along axes of differentiation which organize social formations are the more micro contexts of, for example, specific families or specific workplaces and occupations. These too need to be recognized as the contexts in which archaeological cross-readings such as those proposed by Scott, Mohanty and Henderson occur.

It seems to me that there are three areas which are of particular interest in this cross-reading. First, there is the question of the processes by which concrete historical subjects are created and the place of 'experience' in that context. Second, there is the issue deriving from Mohanty's concern about what happens when 'experience' is tied to issues of 'race' and racism (as well as gender, sexuality, class), i.e. what happens when the category is 'coloured'. Third, there is the issue of the relation between multivocality and the fluid positioning which black female social workers occupy.

Scott's argument is that 'what counts as experience is neither self-evident nor straightforward; it is always contested, always therefore political' (1992: 37), and that to think of it in this way 'does not undercut politics by denying the existence of subjects, it instead interrogates the processes of their creation' (p. 38). This immediately opens up the possibility of thinking about the 'subject of experience' as at once shifting and multiple because she stands at the intersections of complex webs of relations organized around numerous axes of power and differentiation. While rooted in the terrain established by feminist constructions and valorizations of the category, it points a way out of the totalizing and universalist formulations of 'women's experience' common to early second-wave white (and western) feminists. For while it demands that the experience which is spoken is heard, it also demands that the circumstances of that speaking are excavated and analysed.

Most of the speakers considered here proceed in such a way that 'experience' is taken as the starting point of explanation. It is precisely the ontological or foundational status of their collective 'experience' which confirms the importance of employing black women social workers in Social Services departments. This 'experience' is said to produce an understanding, or form of knowledge, about the dynamics of racism (and class) and oppression both historically and contemporarily, which much of the client base will be familiar with. 'Experience' becomes the connective tissue binding social workers and clients and it is this which is vital for Social Services departments. Their employment is an occupational and professional necessity based on a perspective of 'who feels it knows it'. At this level the women speaking here reproduce a way of thinking about and using 'experience' which both Scott and Mohanty critique. But I want to argue that if we take to their logical conclusion their injunctions to interpret and locate 'experience' in light of the web of relations which produce it, then the voices of these women suggest a more complex use of the category. This is precisely because it is a situated use.

The women were attempting to construct their own specificity in the context of a set of questions about their employment. Being asked these questions by a black woman interlocutor ostensibly established an interaction in which the categories 'black woman' and 'black women's experience' needed no preliminary introduction. But even in these conditions, and perhaps because of them, a more complex mobilization of the category 'experience' occurred. For I would suggest that while there was a harmony of voices constructing a unitary 'black women's experience', many also spoke as if they had a peripheral vision of the contingent nature of 'experience' and its complex gendered, 'raced' and classed production. One speaker referred to the realization that her institutional location results in her having a different set of 'experiences' from those with whom she had ertswhile constructed a community. This distancing arises because her location in 'race', gender and class relations becomes reconfigured, a process which is both unavoidable and painful to her. This is similar to another speaker, who seeks a 'way out' of this 'dilemma of distance' by privileging early 'experiences' of oppression, relative poverty, etc., and thus creating a legitimacy and specificity for black female social workers.

This would suggest that if we are to adopt the approach urged by both Scott and Mohanty, three further questions have to be asked: (1) What is it that speakers are attempting to achieve by the invocation of a particular foundational 'experience'? (2) Who is it that is invoking this 'experience'? and (3) Who are they speaking to? When this is done, awareness of the contingent, produced nature of 'experience' may well be implicit in any given sequence of talk, but is subordinated to what is seen as a more urgent imperative. It is only by applying Scott and Mohanty's theoretical positions to concrete, but none the less historical subjects, that this concept can be grasped.

If black female social workers were using a foundational 'experience' to authorize their role and place in Social Services departments they were doing so in an environment in which racism within their workplaces was once again coming to the fore. After an initial 'heyday' in the 1980s when recruitment of black staff to qualified social work positions was a priority in some authorities, the situation in the 1990s is much altered. For example, the 1991 Social Services Inspectorate report on *Women in the Social Services* noted both that despite a recognition of the need for a multi-ethnic social work corps, black social workers were often viewed as a problem rather than an asset, and that black women seldom achieved managerial positions because of pervasive racism and sexism. As Community Care (1993) noted, when black women do enter managerial positions within their departments,

> they are particularly exposed and isolated, and the institutions are slow to support them – worse, their performance is expected to be peerless. On the converse, there are many 'over-qualified' and experienced black workers, able to perform at higher levels, but discouraged within their organisations which go on to reinforce this perception of 'difficult people'.
>
> (p. 14)

All black workers are affected by the upsurge in racism and one of the measures of this is the demise in the numbers of black people at senior management levels in Social Services departments. In this context the 'coloured' or 'raced' nature of the 'experience' constructed by the women speaking here is not at all surprising. It is given a foundational status precisely because it is this which can provide the specificity of the contribution they can offer. They do not become 'good' social workers because of the technical or professional training they receive, but rather because this is mapped on to a subject who understands the client base of social work.

However, recourse to a foundational 'experience' also serves another purpose in this context. By constructing a historical continuity between themselves and previous generations of 'fighters' and 'survivors' they find a way through and a meaning to their working lives. These subjects are then located in an institutional context in which the intersections of 'race', racism and gender are such that their claims to a professional status and competence are being undermined as departments reorganize in the wake of welfare restructuring and the attack on anti-racism in social work.

If this provides the context for this group of black women's multivocality other issues still arise. One of these is related to the totalizing effects which result from privileging 'race'. Because of the closures and erasures which the metalanguage of 'race' can impose, we need a way out by which it is possible to capture some of the complexities and points of difference which can be at work *within* the dominant binaries which have organized meaning for people's everyday lives. Henderson's notion of multivocality or simultaneity of discourse begins this process because it enables us to situate the voices which engage multiple interlocutors in one and the same moment.

For Henderson, black women's speech/writing is profoundly and self-consciously relational but it is this in both an *inter*-relational sense and an *intra*-relational sense. For the simultaneity of discourse through which black women create themselves and claim the space from which to speak is directed to an external and internal same/other. 'What distinguishes black women's writing, then, is the privileging (rather than repressing) of "the other in ourselves"' (1992: 147), and in moving into this speaking position she disrupts the 'intervention by the other(s) who speak for and about black women' (p. 151). To enable this 'dialogue of difference and dialectic of identity . . . black women must speak in a plurality of voices as well as in a multiplicity of discourses' (p. 149), they must, as Henderson says, 'speak in tongues'. Black women's discourses are both testimonial and contestatory because her interlocutors are comprised of a range of same/other(s) organized across numerous axes of differentiation and power.

> Through the multiple voices that enunciate her complex subjectivity, the black woman . . . not only speaks familiarly in the discourse of other(s), but as Other she is in contestorial dialogue with the hegemonic dominant and subdominant or 'ambiguously (non)hegemonic' discourses . . . As such, black women . . . enter into testimonial discourse with black men as blacks, with white women as women, and with black women as black women. At the same time, they enter into a competitive discourse with black men as women, with white women as blacks, and with white men as black women. If black women speak a discourse of racial and gendered difference in the dominant or hegemonic discursive order, they speak a discourse of racial and gender identity and difference in the sub-dominant discursive order.
>
> (Henderson, 1992: 148)

As 'speaking subjects', then, black women in their multiple selves move within and across discourses as they communicate in modes of identification and differentiation with those who constitute an element of themselves.

The voices of these black female social workers offer a clear example of such multivocality in a specific occupational setting. One aspect of their occupational situatedness is that the audiences to whom they are speaking are predominantly white women – as colleagues, managers and in some cases organizational subordinates. Because social work is such a highly gendered occupation, white (and to some extent black) men will also constitute the audiences to whom these women are speaking, but these men will seldom occupy subordinate organizational positions to them. It is this aspect of Social Services departments as gendered domains which in part will account for the marked emphasis in the extracts on the differences between black and white women. They do this by drawing on the discursive repertoires available. As we have seen, some of these involve a collective historical and contemporary 'experience' of racist exclusions and marginalizations occurring outside of the employment context. These 'memories' and 'experiences' are invoked to make sense of the work situation but are of course mediated by the occupational situatedness in which they are mobilized. A second aspect of this occupational situatedness is provided by professional discourses about the nature of social work, for example, the frequent references to social work as being about caring, support, help, imparting life skills and so on. In this sense it is clear that the speakers were drawing on a link between a discursively constituted 'black women's experience' and professional discourses as opposed to the situation they find themselves in organizationally, a situation which they feel undermines and devalues them. The result is that their recourse to a set of professional discourses has to be read in the wider context of their racialized and gendered positioning.

This is part of the 'multivocality' or 'simultaneity of discourse' that these black women adopt. Moreover, in terms of organizational situatedness they do so from a position where they are unambiguously subordinate. However, it is also clear that as black women *social workers* they have statutory and organizational power in relation to *clients*, the great majority of whom are white and black women. In this sense they can occupy a position of being 'ambiguously (non)hegemonic'. It will be remembered that in noting the constituencies to whom black women speak their 'simultaneity of discourse', Henderson always positioned black women as in either a relation of identity or difference but never as in any form of dominance. It is clear that in the case of social workers such a formulation cannot be sustained. And in the accounts given here I would argue that the speakers' claim to professional authority through the mapping of 'black women's experience' on to professional discourse constitutes them as at once organizationally subordinate and ambiguously (non)hegemonic. This can only be gleaned by 'locating the politics of experience'.

Notes

Gail Lewis is a lecturer in social policy at the Open University and a member of the *Feminist Review* Collective.

Many thanks for the generosity of all those women who were willing to talk to her about their working lives. She would also like to thank Annie Whitehead for her invaluable and thoughtful editorial comments. John Clarke, Liliane Landor and Catherine Hall have also provided endless amounts of encouragement and stimulation for which she thanks them.

References

ANZALDUA, G. and **MORAGA, C.** (1983) editors, *This Bridge Called My Back* New York: Kitchen Table: Women of Color Press.
BARRETT, M. and **PHILLIPS, A.** (1992) editors, *Destabilising Theory* Cambridge: Polity Press.
BRYAN, B., DADZIE, S. and **SCAFE, S.** (1985) *The Heart of the Race* London: Virago.

BROOKS-HIGGINBOTHOM, E. (1992) 'The meta-language of race' *Signs*, Vol. 17, No. 2.

BUTLER, J. and SCOTT, J. (1992) editors, *Feminists Theorise the Political* New York and London: Routledge; reprinted from **WALL, C. A.** (1991) editor, *Changing our Own Worlds* New Brunswick: Rutgers University Press.

CARBY, H. V. (1982) 'White woman listen! black feminism and the boundaries of sisterhood' in Centre for Contemporary Cultural Studies *The Empire Strikes Back* London: Hutchinson.

CHOONG, D., COLEWILSON, O., PARKER, S. and PEARSE, G. (1991) editors, *Don't Ask Me Why: An Anthology of Short Stories by Black Women* London: Black Women Talk.

COMMUNITY CARE (1993) 20 May, pp. 14–15.

DALLEY, G. (1988) *Ideologies of Caring: Rethinking Community and Collectivism* London: Macmillan.

FEMINIST REVIEW (1984) 'Many voices: one chant', 17.

GREWAL, S., KAY, J., LANDOR, L., LEWIS, G. and PARMAR, P. (1987) *Charting the Journey* London: Sheba Feminist Press.

GRIMWOOD, C. and POPPLESTONE, R. (1993) editors, *Women, Management and Care* Basingstoke: Macmillan.

HENDERSON, M. G. (1992) 'Speaking in tongues: dialogics, dialectics and the black woman writer's literary tradition' in **Butler** and **Scott**, editors; first published in C. A. Wall (1991) editor, *Changing Our Own Worlds* New Brunswick, Rutgers University Press.

HULL, G., BELL SCOTT, P. and SMITH, B. (1982) editors, *All the Women are White, All the Blacks are Men, But Some of us are Brave* New York: Feminist Press.

JORDAN, J. (1986) *On Call: Political Essays* London and Sydney: Pluto.

JOYCE, P. (1994) *Democratic Subjects: The Self and The Social in Nineteenth Century England* Cambridge: Cambridge University Press.

LORDE, A. (1984) *SisterOutsider* New York: The Crossing Press.

MOHANTY, C. Talpade (1992) 'Feminist encounters: locating the politics of experience' in **Barrett** and **Phillips**, editors.

PAINTER, N. (1995) *Soul Murder: African-American Slave Families* Paper presented to the XVIIIth Congress of Historical Studies, August, Montreal.

PARMAR, P. (1982) 'Gender, race and class: Asian women in resistance' Centre for Contemporary Cultural Studies *The Empire Strikes Back* London: Hutchinson.

RICH, A. (1984) 'Notes towards a politics of location' *Blood, Bread and Poetry: Selected Prose 1979–1985* New York: W. W. Norton & Company.

ROJEK, C., PEACOCK, G. and COLLINS, S. (1988) *Social Work and Received Ideas* London: Routledge & Kegan Paul.

SCOTT, J. (1992) 'Experience' in **Butler and Scott, editors**.

SMITH, B. (1982) 'Towards a black feminist criticism' in **Hull, Bell Scott** and **Smith**, editors.

—— (1983) editor, *Home Girls: A Black Feminist Anthology* New York: Kitchen Table: Women of Color Press.

SOCIAL SERVICES INSPECTORATE (1991) *Women in the Social Services* (Department of Health) London: HMSO.
SULTER, M. (1990) editor, *Passion: Discourses on Black Women's Creativity* Hebden Bridge: Urban Fox Press.
WANDOR, M. (1990) *Once A Feminist: Stories of a Generation* London: Virago.

Insider Perspectives or Stealing the Words out of Women's Mouths:
Interpretation in the Research Process

Diane Reay

Abstract

This article examines the ways in which social class differences between the researcher and female respondents affect data analysis. I elaborate the ways in which my class background, just as much as my gender, affects all stages of the research process from theoretical starting points to conclusions. The influences of reflexivity, power and 'truth' on the interpretative process are developed by drawing on fieldnotes and interviews from an ethnographic study of women's involvement in their children's primary schooling. Complexities of social class are explored both in relation to myself as the researcher and to how the women saw themselves. I argue that there is a thin dividing line between the understandings which similar experiences of respondents bring to the research process and the element of exploitation implicit in mixing up one's own personal history with those of women whose experience of the same class is very different. Identification can result in a denial of the power feminist researchers exercise in the selection and interpretation of data. However, researchers are similarly powerful in relation to women from very different class backgrounds to their own, and I attempt to draw out problematic issues around power and 'truth' in relation to the middle-class women whom I interviewed. I conclude by reiterating that, from where I am socially positioned, certain aspects of the data are much more prominent than others and as a consequence interpretation remains an imperfect and incomplete process.

Keywords

feminism; social class; reflexivity; power; difference; interpretation

Introduction

As part of my doctoral research, I interviewed thirty-three women whose 10-year-old children attended two socially contrasting, urban primary schools. Milner is a multi-ethnic, predominantly working-class school in inner London. Oak Park, three miles to the north of Milner, has a largely white, middle-class intake. My sample reflected the maternal population in the two schools and constituted a diverse group of black, white and mixed-race working- and middle-class women. One-third of my sample were lone mothers, while the rest were either cohabiting or married to their male partners. My research looked at gender inequalities operating within families in relation to involvement in children's schooling (Reay, 1995a). However, I also wanted to examine the impact of differences among women on their relationship to their children's schooling. While I felt that I explored differences of 'race', ethnicity and marital status fairly unproblematically, it was in relation to social class differences that tensions arose both in my relationship with women in the field (Reay, 1995b) and in my interpretation of what they said. In this article I look at how social class differences both between myself and the respondents and among the women themselves affected data analysis. I also focus on issues of reflexivity, power and 'truth', and the complex ways in which they impact upon the interpretative process.

Women and social class

Raising issues of social class within feminism always feels like either an act of disloyalty or a display of ignorance. As recent post-structuralist debates both within and outside feminism have made clear, social class categories fail to capture the complexities of contemporary social life (Barrett, 1991; 1992). However, social class continues to be one of the major filters through which individuals make sense of the world. Until more complex ways of understanding economic inequalities are developed which match the complex theorizations of gender inequalities available, many feminists such as myself will continue to struggle with the concept in their work.

Within my doctoral thesis I theorize social class as process. I have attempted, through a focus on the processes of maternal activities, to demonstrate a different way of envisaging social class, one that allows for deeper, more complexly shaded analyses than a monochromatic map of social class location provides. However, I also wanted to explore where the women position themselves in terms of social class. All the women were asked at the end of the interview to describe their social class position. In addition to self-assignation, I also collected information on educational qualifications, income level, housing tenure and occupations, past and present.

Pierre Bourdieu talks of the boundaries between social classes as 'flames whose edges are in constant movement' (Bourdieu, 1987: 13). All the Oak Park mothers, apart from Maureen who told me without hesitation that she was working class, described their own parents as middle class and saw their current status as middle class. However, in the Milner sample there was much flickering around the edges. The black mothers of the teenage girls whom Heidi Mirza interviewed had occupations such as social worker, nurse and teacher but they would be categorized as working class because their male partners were employed in skilled and semi-skilled manual work. However, as Mirza points out, the reality is more complex (Mirza, 1992). In Milner, Lelia, Jalil, Linda, Bo and Oya all came from middle-class backgrounds. However, for Bo, Jalil and Oya issues centring around 'race', geography, immigrant status and current impoverishment led them to question the relevance of middle-class labels in understanding their present situation. In fact Jalil was quite adamant that she was working class in spite of her parents' middle-class status prior to emigrating to Britain.

The other fifteen mothers in Milner all came from working-class backgrounds. However, five of these women expressed ambivalence about their social class position. While they shared similar class backgrounds with the other ten women, their self-identity had subsequently been shaped by different educational trajectories to that of the others; ones which had been affected by a degree of educational success. For Anita, as a black woman with a nursing qualification, her current occupational status gave rise to feelings of ambiguity about her social class. She talked in terms of coming from a working-class background but 'not really being working class now'.

There were thus eight women whose relationship to social class was characterized by ambivalences and ambiguities, the consequences of having to deal with very different circumstances to the ones in which they had grown up. Three were coping with the difficulty of reconciling a middle-class background with current impoverishment while the other five, including Anita, were dealing with a changing sense of self, resulting from educational and/or career success and how that interacted with the influences of a working-class background. The ambiguities of Oya's social status are captured in her words: 'I suppose I am middle class, but middle class living in a council flat on a working-class income.' Christine told me: 'I don't like to think in terms of class. I mean we're all much the same now. I prefer to think of myself as classless.' Bo commented: 'I'm poor. I think that's the most important thing. I may have a middle-class background but at the moment I'm poor and that's the most important thing about my life.' Ann, who shares a very similar background to my own, laughed: 'I don't know really. We are certainly not well off. Like we were saying it's difficult for a coal-miner's daughter to call herself middle class.'

These women seemed to inhabit 'the oscillating borderland between classes' (Bourdieu, 1987: 13). While Oya and Bo entered into a discourse of 'middle class but . . .', the other five women resisted class labels because they recognized the uncertain, shifting territory they occupied; a class landscape of 'maybe' and 'perhaps' where personal history shaped current consciousness and where there were none of the certainties of conventional middle-class horizons. It was a landscape I felt familiar with. As is evident throughout the rest of this article, much of my time in the research field was caught up in an attempt to reconcile my own working-class past with a middle-class present. The conflict inherent in such multiple positionings spilled over into both the interviewing process and the interpretation of my data.

Reflexivity

In their article 'Coming to conclusions: power and interpretation in researching young women's sexuality', Janet Holland and Caroline Ramazanoglu state that:

> By treating coming to conclusions as a social process, we can show that interpretation is a political, contested and unstable process between the lives of the researchers and those of the researched. Interpretation needs somehow to unite a passion for 'truth' with explicit rules of research method that can make some conclusions stronger than others.
> (Holland and Ramazanoglu, 1994: 127)

I have struggled to adopt their suggested principles in my own process of data analysis both by making clear my epistemological position and by recognizing my role in the research process. Reflexivity, in the sense of a continual consideration of the ways in which the researcher's own social identity and values affect the data gathered and the picture of the social world produced, has been a paramount project within feminism. Feminist researchers have stressed the importance of locating themselves within their research (Gelsthorpe, 1992; McRobbie, 1982; Maynard and Purvis, 1994; Roberts, 1981; Walkerdine and Lucey, 1989). In *Breaking Out Again* Liz Stanley and Sue Wise argue that: 'recognition that who a researcher is, in terms of their sex, race, class and sexuality, affects what they "find" in research is as true for feminist as any other researchers' (Stanley and Wise, 1993: 228).

My own research study draws on the theoretical framework of Pierre Bourdieu and I have used feminist writing as a foil to Bourdieu's own position on reflexivity in the research process. For Bourdieu:

> Reflexivity is not achieved by the use of the first person or by the expedient of constructing a text which situates the observer in the act of observation. Rather it is achieved by subjecting the *position* of the observer to the same critical analysis as that of the constructed object at hand.
>
> (Barnard, 1990: 75)

Bourdieu and Wacquant argue that reflexivity entails breaking with 'spontaneous representations in currency in the intellectual world' (Bourdieu and Wacquant, 1992: 88). But what of the female research student in her forties who is positioned as relatively powerless in the intellectual world; whose feminism, working-class background and political commitments lead her to reject these 'spontaneous representations in currency in the intellectual world'? It is eminent, white, male professors of sociology, with an enormous corpus of intellectual theorizing, who need to heed his advice. He is writing for himself, not for me. I continually have to explain myself in my texts, to write my difference in. It is male stream academics, who take their position for granted, who consequently need to engage in a process of becoming aware of the partiality of their theories.

In contrast, I am all too aware of my own complex social positioning and its effects on the research process. At the end of May 1992, one month after starting my Ph.D., I wrote in my research diary:

> One of my main preliminary concerns is whether my subjectivity as an educated working-class woman will prevent me from embracing a wider perspective than my own class, 'race' and gender bound preconceptions. My subjectivity becomes problematic in a way that middle-class women's would not. I feel it is increasingly acceptable to adopt a feminist stance in academic research. There exists no paradigm for a working class stance. To what extent is the term a nonsense? What have the working class to do with the academy? I feel caught in a conundrum. One possible way out is to use the research process as a means of questioning the view of knowledge which sees it as hierarchical.
>
> (30 May 1992)

Kathleen Lynch and Cathleen O'Neill maintain that, while other oppressed groups do not lose their minority defining status through becoming educated, if working-class people become educated they cease to be working class, at least to a degree. They conclude that the relationship between social class and education is fundamentally different from that of gender and 'race': 'While we have feminist and racially informed visions of education, there is no working-class perspective' (Lynch and O'Neill, 1994: 321). They argue that working-class knowledge is viewed as inferior and inadmissible by intellectuals; always at the bottom of any hierarchy of knowledge.

Power and telling the 'truth'

Over three years and more than five hundred academic books and articles later, I have come back full circle to my original question of hierarchies of knowledge. The issue is still an uncomfortable one, but this time I am positioned differently, as the researcher with access to more 'valued' knowledge than that of the women I have interviewed. How do I escape the hierarchies of knowledge? bell hooks suggests that one strategy is to learn to 'separate useful knowledge you may get from the dominating group, from participation in ways of knowing that would lead to estrangement, alienation, and worse – assimilation and co-optation (1990: 150). However, the seductions of 'knowing better' rather than *knowing differently* are ever present.

Data analysis and interpretation is frequently written up as a complex and difficult intellectual process. If you are drawing on pre-existing theoretical frameworks, which concepts do you adopt and which do you need to adapt? How do you make judgements about whether your data fits the theoretical frame? If you are using grounded theory, which are the significant themes and how do they interrelate? When do you reach the point of theoretical saturation? (Glaser and Strauss, 1967).[1] However, what I did not find in the methods texts was any elaboration of the researcher's power in relation to, first, selecting which data to use, and second, how these data are interpreted. Throughout the research process, I have felt a continuing unease because I have had to deal with a paradoxical tension. Like many other feminists I chose to do research which was central to my own experience. My fear of distorting the often similar experiences of the women whom I interviewed generated a constant sense of insecurity which in turn served to underline my power as interpreter. Barbara Du Bois has outlined the dangers of proximity:

> The closer our subject matter to our own life and experience, the more we can probably expect our own beliefs about the world to enter into and shape our work – to influence the very questions we pose, our conception of how to approach those questions, and the interpretations we generate from our findings.
>
> (Du Bois 1983: 105)

These feelings were intensified because at root my research is advocacy research. I have a message I want to tell: that there are myriad injustices that are being perpetrated and they are not all gendered. They are often racial and are frequently related to age and sexuality, but they can also be the consequences of women's activities; more specifically the activities of privileged women which have negative reverberations on the lives of less privileged women. That my social positioning, past and present, should powerfully influence my perspective is unsurprising. As Elizabeth Wheatley points out:

> Ethnographic relations, practices and representations, as well as the metaphors we use to make sense of them, are *contextually contingent* – their character is shaped by *who* we look at, from *where* we look, and *why* we are looking in the first place.
>
> (Wheatley, 1994: 422, my emphasis)

However, uncovering the power that some women have relative to others has been paralleled by a sense of the increasing visibility of my own power in selecting and interpreting the data.

A major difficulty in interpreting the data lay in the contesting versions of 'truth' circulating throughout society. Neither my 'truth' nor those of the working-class women I interviewed fit easily into academic 'truths'. In a world where there are hierarchies of knowledge, what I learned as a working-class child has always been relegated to the realms of the intuitive; it has never counted as knowledge. That the middle classes are imbued with a sense of their own intrinsic superiority is not something I need to read about, or develop an awareness of. The knowledge comes directly out of my experience as a working-class child and young woman, except that now I can read it in my data. It is there in middle-class women's words and in their children's behaviour in the classrooms (Reay, 1995c; 1995d). Although, in the 1950s and 1960s such knowledge was the subject of male, left academic writing (Hoggart, 1957; Jackson and Marsden, 1966), it is now rarely problematized in academic theory, irrespective of the gender of the author. Academia is a social location where particular 'truths' are told (Walkerdine, 1990). As Bourdieu asserts in his inaugural lecture, the sociologist may acquire that special insight associated with every kind of social displacement only by refusing to accept both 'the populist representation of the people, which deceives only those who create it, and the élitist representation of the élite, neatly made to deceive those who are in it and those who are not' (Bourdieu, quoted in Duncan, 1990: 181).

Following on from this it is clear that my espousal of a commitment to challenging, working and writing to counter inequalities will only amount to so many empty words if it is not underpinned by a recognition of my current situation where I am now in a position of power; of 'class', as well as of 'race', privilege. Just as bell hooks points out that the very light skinned black woman, by having the ability to pass as white, has access to a totally different perspective on 'race' from someone who is dark skinned and will never pass (hooks, 1984), so I now have the ability to pass as middle class. My perspective on social class can no longer claim to be that of the working-class woman who has not experienced the advantages which accrue through higher education. However, that is not the same as saying that my working-class background does not effect the research process. It generates both negative and positive effects. First, because I can never quite escape the confines of the dominant, sociological discourses that I am struggling against, I find it difficult not to view my working-class history as a problem to be controlled. From it stems my particular, emotive 'non-intellectual' responses, my bias, my partiality. In other moments I recognize it as a strength. Voices that are informed by insider knowledge of working-class culture rarely inform academic writing. My experiences of growing up as working class differed from those of the women I interviewed in terms of either ethnicity, generation or geography and sometimes all three. However, the contribution of shared understandings, of shared views about the world and our place within it, has always been seen as a resource in feminist research. I found I still shared more with the working- than the middle-class women, in spite of my current position of privilege.

The thin dividing line between identification and exploitation

Holland and Ramazanoglu write:

> Even if the researcher identifies politically *with* women, this does not necessarily give us the methodological tools with which to avoid the conceptual distancing of women from their experience.
>
> (Holland and Ramazanoglu, 1994: 126–7)

Holland and Ramazanoglu's study was, in fact, research into the sexuality of young women and men. However, while they raise the issue of power in interpretation, they do not discuss the possible effects of having a greater political commitment to the women they interviewed than to the men. Distancing operates on two levels. The conceptual distancing Holland and Ramazanoglu write about is a consequence of sociological discourses being located within the 'relations of ruling' (Smith, 1989). Theorizing women's experiences invariably means adopting a very different perspective to the respondent's own. I would also suggest that it is problematic for feminist researchers to try and find a space between theoretical standpoints which does not address the specificities of their own experience. The end result could be the objectification of both themselves and the women they interview.

But what of the woman researcher, who identifies with some of the women in her research and not others? Janet Holland and Caroline Ramazanoglu also hint earlier in their article at a second distancing, the distancing of the researcher from the researched, which results in their inscription as 'other'. I realize that to an extent I have made middle-class women 'the other' of my research. This has come about because, as well as having a theoretical focus on inequalities, I found myself identifying far more strongly with the concerns and perspectives about the education of their children of both the working-class women and the women who felt ambivalent about their social class status than with those of the middle-class women.

Joanne Braxton, describing her responses to other black women's autobiographies, writes, 'I read every text through my own experience, as well as the experiences of my mother and my grandmothers' (Braxton, 1989: 1). The affirmation of finding myself at the core of some women's accounts contains enormous power. I can read my centrality where so often there has only been my partiality. However, increasingly, I have come to recognize this centrality as a strength only when it is embedded in an understanding of the weaknesses associated with being centre stage. It is no less a position of limited vision than standing in the wings. As a consequence, I have come to view my interpretation of working-class women's accounts as holding the dangers of proximity rather than distance. I often found myself feeling angry when listening to them speak. I felt angry about the many tales of horrendous school experiences, at repeated, unsuccessful attempts to be heard by school personnel, and concerns about their children's undemanding curriculum. I then had to address the issue of whether I was conflating their many varied experiences with my own. Was I finding in the field the slights, rejections and silencings I had experienced in my own educational career? There is a thin dividing line between the understandings that similar experiences of respondents bring to the research process and the element of exploitation implicit in mixing up one's own personal history with very different working-class experiences.

Dealing with difficult differences

In her article 'Qualitative research, appropriation of the "other" and empowerment' Anne Opie raises questions about feminist interpretations. She writes that:

> Although at one point they are liberatory because they open to inspection what has been previously hidden, they are also restrictive in the sense that they can appropriate the data to the researcher's interests, so that other significant experiential elements which challenge or partially disrupt that interpretation can be silenced.
>
> (Opie, 1992: 52)

In order to illustrate imperfections in the interpretative process, I have selected some data that I had not adequately dealt with in my conclusions. In the course of interviewing Lisa, the single parent of a very bright, white, working-class girl, she told me, 'I don't care what Lucy does, she can be a road sweeper for all I care, just as long as she's happy.' I can recall intellectually flinching. I realized later, as I was transcribing the tape, that I had not accepted her comment because I suggested that Lucy is clever enough to go to university. In retrospect I was doubly uneasy about Lisa's words, first, because they have nothing to do with my experience of being working class; working-class experience is not monolithic. Second, her version does not allow me to say what I want to say about working-class women's aspirations for their children.

As an attempt to deal with this in my preliminary conclusions I have written 'all the working-class women, except one . . .'. In writing this I realize my interpretation is all about my acculturation and very little about Lisa's words. I have become too entwined in academia to fight my way clear of the values I have internalized. My immediate pejorative response is still there months later. Since then I have gone back to the transcripts of Lisa's interview. Now my reading is different. Although Lisa's views on the irrelevance of social status and her lack of ambition for her daughter do not readily fit into my initial analysis, they have a powerful coherence within her own philosophical framework, which holds that ultimately the most important thing is to be a good person, who above all values connection with friends, relatives and neighbours. She displays a counter-hegemonic value system: the challenge to notions of individualism and private property, which bell hooks describes in *Talking Back* (hooks, 1989). Within her framework individual failure has nothing to do with educational qualifications. There are many related comments to support her first statement, which remain uncoded in the transcripts. She talks of the stereotyping of the ignorant: 'Do the ignorant ever look around London when they talk about inner cities? Everywhere is so different, they talk as if it's all the same, when really it's such a mixture. They never seem to see that there's a lot of good people out there.' In imposing my feminist standpoint on what Lisa said, I had either omitted her challenges to dominant discourses or reduced them to irrelevancies and false consciousness. The ignorant for Lisa include academics. They trade in irrelevancies, not her. My interpretation denies her her subversive reading of the *status quo*. And these are the women on whose side I see myself as being!

But what of the middle-class women I interviewed? Holland and Ramazanoglu stress that 'We cannot read meaning *in* interview texts, allowing them to propose their own meanings, without also reading meaning *into* them, as we make sense of their meanings' (Holland and Ramazanoglu, 1994: 133). I read both assumption and denial of privilege in the middle-class women's transcripts but what would the feminist researcher from a different social location make of my data? My doctoral research is about mothers' involvement in their children's education. Pamela told me:

> 'I think the most important thing as a mother is to be supportive. I don't think it matters whether you have got a lot of specific knowledge, what's important is to allow your child to feel you are interested in whatever they are doing. It does not matter how academically knowledgeable you are. What's important is that when they want to tell you about it you are there to listen.'

In Pamela's account material and academic advantages do not count. Instead what makes a difference is the availability of the mother. On one level I have no problem with her thesis that it is important to listen to children, to hear what they are saying. But there are competing versions coming out of what working-class women were telling me. For them, material and academic resources did make a significant difference. I would suggest that they do not figure in Pamela's account because she can take them for granted. She has a first degree, an MA and her family income is over £40,000 a year. I see in her words an implicit denial of her own advantage and concomitantly, other women's disadvantage. This difficulty, that many of the middle-class women had in owning their privilege, was there in the silences, omissions and contradictions in their transcripts. Although the research focus was clearly on support for schooling I only found out about two children's weekly private tuition sessions through my participant observation in the classroom. Only one middle-class mother told me about her au pair, but from children's discussions in the playground I discovered over half the women had au pairs, cleaners or both. It was the recognition of what middle-class women were omitting which led to a parallel process of identifying the silence in all the white women's transcripts, namely any admission or understanding of the advantages of their 'whiteness' (Frankenberg, 1993).

My feminism has been central to all aspects of the research process. When I have been analysing and interpreting women's relationships with men, the process of going beyond what women actually say has not been problematic because I find myself in the familiar terrain of feminist theory. However, drawing out differences between women, specifically in relation to social class, is a totally different proposition in an academic climate in which Michelle Barrett writes, 'social class is definitely non grata as a topic' (Barrett, 1992). I find myself in a very different area of feminist theory, where there continue to be deep-seated problems around theorizing the power relations between women. Yet, as I have described earlier, my class background, just as much as my gender, affects all stages of the research process from theoretical starting point to my conclusions. Why am I utilizing Bourdieu's conceptual framework rather than Foucault's, whom so many feminists have worked with? Because his work makes direct links between issues of power and domination and social class. The other theorist, whose theoretical framework I am employing in my research, is Dorothy Smith, not just because of her powerful feminist theory, but also because she is centrally concerned with issues of class (Smith, 1983; 1988).

Social class similarly effects my own part in the research process (Reay, 1995b, 1996). But, and here I feel in much more unfamiliar and unsafe territory, it clearly influences what I hold to be 'true'. I find myself still with the dilemma of the working-class stance as when I started the research process. Only now it is shaky and contestable because, as I predicted over three years ago, there is no place for it in academia. I now identify myself as middle class although I often try and explain that I have not always been thus. The process through which working-class women experience higher education inevitably disconnects them from their social origins and proffers new, seductive allegiances. Maintaining the connection means a very careful listening to what black and white working-class women are saying. That is not the same as always taking what they say at face value. As Kum Kum Bhavnani asserts, there are other ways of treating what respondents say seriously (Bhavnani, 1993). What I suggest it does mean is never to assume a superior knowledge. Being middle class means knowing different, not better, things. It constitutes another partiality.

Towards the end of my fieldwork I interviewed a middle-class woman called Alice. After a few minutes of talking with her I realized, with dawning horror, that we shared the same schooling, but very different experiences of it. Describing her own schooling she told me:

> 'I quite enjoyed primary school actually. I felt I could achieve. I think one was quite frightened by the teachers but because I came top it was not too much of a problem. I did enjoy helping the children who were trailing. When I'd finished my work I was always allowed to help those children who were behind. That was nice but I used to get mortified. Most of the children were from mining families and so they were seen as dirty, smelly children. When they were ridiculed or poked fun at I used to get angry. It makes me sound like a goody-goody but that was the case.'

How do I interpret a text in which as a coal-miner's daughter I am so clearly positioned as 'the other'? I found myself recoiling at being the 'dirty, smelly' in Alice's account but said nothing until I discovered we had both attended the same girls' grammar school. I mention that I also went to Montgrove, but I tell her nothing about my class background. Alice recounts how she became the rebel, speaking out on behalf of all the girls who were too intimidated by the authoritarian regime to find a voice. I do not tell her I hardly said a word throughout my secondary schooling. Neither do I tell her that my experience of that middle-class girls' grammar school was that no one spoke for me, nor do I reveal that, in my view, she was only speaking for herself. Joan Acker, Kate Barry and Johanna Esseveld highlight the ethical dilemmas confronting feminist researchers when faced with women whose interpretation of their lives diverges radically from their own (Acker *et al.*, 1991). However, now I have the power to decide both whether she should have a voice in my text and how that voice should be framed.

Although initially I was tempted to leave Alice's words out of my analysis, it is clear that any interpretation which seeks to reveal the contribution of personal history to current positions of privilege needs to work with her account, however uncomfortable it makes me as the researcher feel. At least issues around class and inequality are there in this middle-class woman's account. They go unmentioned in other privileged women's transcripts, as invisible as 'race' is in the white women's interviews. The taken-for-granted of the socially privileged spans gender, 'race' *and* class. Interpreting the accounts of the privileged needs to be rooted first in a questioning of the construction of difference as either deficit or denial of dis/advantage (Walkerdine and Lucey, 1989), and second, in a commitment to making visible what the limited vision of centrality hides (hooks, 1989).

The problems I faced in analysing accounts like Lisa's and Alice's led me to rethink my conceptual framework. I began to feel that the idea of cultural capital (Bourdieu, 1984) with which I had originally started out did not sufficiently capture the complexities of either these women's lives or my own. Half-way through the process of data analysis I again started using Bourdieu's less well-known concept of habitus as a way of looking at women (Bourdieu, 1985); a way that conceptualizes the present in terms of the influences of the past, stresses differences within, as well as across, social class groupings, and recognizes the impact of wider social context. Although Bourdieu's concept is primarily linked to social class in his own work, I have attempted to develop understandings of habitus as both gendered and racialized (Reay, 1995c; 1995d). I now feel my interpretative framework provides a more sensitive response to difference, privilege and disadvantage.

However, interpretation remains an imperfect and incomplete process. There are many possible readings of interview transcripts. From where I am socially positioned certain aspects of the data are much more prominent than others. I have wrestled with the conundrum of whether this constitutes an undesirable bias or whether it can lead to a real reflexivity. I have tried to address the difference my difference makes by centring my analysis in feminist understandings of what women share, as well as focusing on the differences between them. In terms of my own research this means continually explicating what mothering entails for women, while highlighting the inequalities all women experience, to differing extents, in their relationships with men. On a fundamental level, searching for inequalities inevitably means finding them. In spite, or perhaps because of this, I would like to make the case that searching out inequalities of all kinds should be integral to feminist methodology. However, as Holland and Ramazanoglu cogently point out, this is not possible unless recognition of power and power dynamics informs our interpretation of research data:

> The validity of our interpretations depends on the integrity of the interaction of our personal experiences with the power of feminist theory and the power, or lack of power, of the researched. Our conclusions should always be open to criticism.
>
> (Holland and Ramazanoglu, 1994: 146)

Notes

Diane Reay worked for twenty years as a teacher in inner London where she was extensively involved in anti-sexist and anti-racist work. In 1995 she completed a Ph.D. on mothers' involvement in their children's primary schooling. She is currently employed as a research associate at King's College, London, where she is researching the impact of market forces in education and issues around gender and coping with cancer.

I would like to thank Annie Whitehead for her support and many insightful comments on an earlier draft of this article.

1 Over recent years there has been a growing body of feminist work which engages with these issues; see, for example, Roberts, 1981; Cook and Fonow, 1986; Fonow and Cook, 1991; Smith, 1988; Devault, 1990; Gelsthorpe, 1990; Maynard and Purvis, 1994.

References

ACKER, Joan, BARRY, Kate and ESSEVELD, Johanna (1991) 'Objectivity and truth: problems in doing feminist research' in **Fonow** and **Cook**, editors.

BARNARD, Henri (1990) 'Bourdieu and ethnography: reflexivity, politics and praxis' in **Harker et al.**, editors.

BARRETT, Michelle (1991) *The Politics of Truth: From Marx to Foucault* Cambridge: Polity Press.

—— (1992) 'Words and things' in **Barrett** and **Phillips**, editors.

BARRETT, M. and PHILLIPS, A. (1992) editors, *Destabilising Theory* London: Polity Press.

BHAVNANI, Kum Kum (1993) 'Tracing the contours of feminist research and feminist objectivity' *Women's Studies International Forum* Vol. 6, No. 2: 95–104.

BOURDIEU, Pierre (1984) *Distinction* London: Routledge & Kegan Paul.

—— (1985) 'The genesis of the concepts of "Habitus" and "Field"' *Sociocriticism* Vol. 2, No. 2: 11–24.

—— (1987) 'What makes a social class? On the theoretical and practical existence of groups' *The Berkeley Journal of Sociology* Vol. 32, No. 1: 1–17.

—— (1993) *Sociology in Question* London: Sage.

BOURDIEU, Pierre and WACQUANT, Loic (1992) *An Invitation to Reflexive Sociology* Chicago: University of Chicago Press.

BOWLES, Gloria and KLEIN, Renate Duelli (1983) editors, *Theories of Women Studies* London: Routledge & Kegan Paul.

BRAXTON, Joanne (1989) *Black Women Writing Autobiography: A Tradition Within a Tradition* Philadelphia: Temple University Press.

COOK, Judith A. and FONOW, Mary Margaret (1986) 'Knowledge and women's interests: issues of epistemology and methodology in feminist sociological research' *Sociological Inquiry* No. 56: 2–29.

DEVAULT, Marjorie (1990) 'Talking and listening from women's standpoint: feminist strategies for interviewing and analysis' *Social Problems* Vol. 37, No. 1: 96–116.

DU BOIS, Barbara (1983) 'Passionate scholarship: notes on values, knowing and method in feminist social science' in **Bowles** and **Klein**, editors.

DUNCAN, Ian (1990) 'Bourdieu on Bourdieu: learning the lesson of the lecon' in **Harker, Mahar** and **Wilkes**, editors.

EDWARDS, R. and RIBBENS, J. (1995) editors, *Women in Families and Households: Qualitative Research. Women's Studies International Forum Special Issue.*

FONOW, Mary Margaret and COOK, Judith (1991) editors, *Beyond Methodology: Feminist Scholarship as Lived Research* Bloomington and Indianapolis: Indiana University Press.

FRANKENBERG, Ruth (1993) *The Social Construction of Whiteness: White Women, Race Matters* London: Routledge.

GELSTHORPE, L. (1990) 'Feminist methodologies in criminology' in **Gelsthorpe** and **Morris**, editors: 213–17.

—— 'Response to Martyn Hammersley's paper on feminist methodology' *Sociology* Vol. 26, No. 2.
GELSTHORPE, L. and MORRIS, A. (1990) editors, *Feminist Perspectives in Criminology* Buckingham: Open University Press.
GLASER, Barney G. and STRAUSS, Anselm L. (1967) *The Discovery of Grounded Theory: Strategies of Qualitative Research* London: Weidenfeld & Nicolson.
GRIFFITHS, M. and TROYNA, B. (1995) editors, *Anti-racism, Culture and Social Justice in Education* London: Trentham Books.
HARKER, R., MAHAR, Cheleen and WILKES, Chris (1990) editors, *An Introduction to the Work of Pierre Bourdieu: The Practice of Theory* London: Macmillan.
HOGGART, Richard (1957) *The Uses of Literacy: Aspects of Working-class Life* London: Chatto & Windus.
HOLLAND, Janet and RAMAZANOGLU, Caroline (1994) 'Coming to conclusions: power and interpretation in researching young women's sexuality' in Maynard and Purvis, editors.
hooks, bell (1984) *Feminist Theory: From Margin to Centre* Boston: South End Press.
—— (1989) *Talking Back: Thinking Feminist – Thinking Black* London: Sheba Feminist Publishers.
—— (1990) *Yearning: Race, Gender and Cultural Politics* London: Turnaround.
JACKSON, Brian and MARSDEN, Dennis (1966) *Education and the Working Class* Harmondsworth: Penguin.
LYNCH, Kathleen and O'NEILL, Cathleen (1994) 'The colonisation of social class in education' *British Journal of Sociology of Education* Vol. 15, No. 3: 307–24.
McROBBIE, Angela (1982) 'The politics of feminist research: between talk, text and action' *Feminist Review* Vol. 12: 46–57.
MAYNARD, Mary and PURVIS, June (1994) editors, *Researching Women's Lives from a Feminist Perspective* London: Taylor & Francis.
MILIBAND, Ralph and SAVILLE, John (1983) editors, *The Socialist Register* London: Merlin Press.
MIRZA, Heidi (1992) *Young, Female and Black* London: Routledge.
OPIE, Anne (1992) 'Qualitative research, appropriation of the "other" and empowerment' *Feminist Review* Vol. 40: 52–69.
REAY, Diane (1995a) 'A silent majority: mothers in parental involvement' in Edwards and Ribbens, editors.
—— (1995b) 'The fallacy of easy access' *Women's Studies International Forum* Vol. 18, No. 1: 205–13.
—— (1995c) 'Using habitus to look at "race" and class in primary school classrooms' in Griffiths and Troyna, editors.
—— (1995d) 'They employ cleaners to do that': habitus in the primary classroom' *British Journal of Sociology of Education* Vol. 16, No. 3: 353–71.
—— (1996) 'Dealing with difficult differences: reflexivity and social class in feminist research' in Walkerdine, editor.

ROBERTS, Helen (1981) editor, *Doing Feminist Research* London: Routledge & Kegan Paul.
SMITH, Dorothy (1983) 'Women, class and family' in **Miliband** and **Saville**, editors.
—— (1988) *The Everyday World as Problematic: A Feminist Sociology* Milton Keynes: Open University Press.
—— (1989) 'Sociological theory: methods of writing patriarchy' in **Wallace**, editor.
STANLEY, Liz and WISE, Sue (1993) *Breaking Out Again: Feminist Ontology and Epistemology* London: Routledge.
WALKERDINE, Valerie (1990) *Schoolgirl Fictions* London: Verso.
—— (1996) editor, *Feminism and Psychology. Special Issue on Social Class.*
WALKERDINE, Valerie and LUCEY, Helen (1989) *Democracy in the Kitchen: Regulating Mothers and Socialising Daughters* London: Virago.
WALLACE, Ruth (1989) editor, *Feminism and Sociological Theory* London: Sage.
WHEATLEY, Elizabeth (1994) 'Dances with feminists: truths, dares and ethnographic stares' *Women's Studies International Forum* Vol. 17, No. 4: 421–3.

Revolutionary Spaces:
Photographs of Working-class Women by Esther Bubley
1940–1943

Jacqueline Ellis

Abstract

This article had several purposes. First, I wanted to highlight the work of Esther Bubley, an American photographer whose documentary work for the Farm Security Administration and the Office of War Information in the early 1940s is largely unknown. Second, I wanted to show how her images complicated and undermined the traditional themes of Depression era photography in the United States. Third, by looking at her images of women, my intention was to reveal how she worked against depictions of femininity during the Depression, and in confrontation with one-dimensional portrayals of women as America entered the Second World War. In conclusion, I contend that Bubley's images were fundamentally portrayals of working-class femininity represented as being an individual – rather than a symbolic – experience. Most specifically in the images I have examined, Bubley deconstructs an ideological image of female working-class identity which was central to documentary photography in 1930s America. For example, unlike in photographs by Dorothea Lange, Bubley did not portray working-class women as metaphoric sites of passive endurance which would eventually lead to the rejuvenation of American nationalism. Rather, she showed working-class women to be potentially subversive in the ways they defined themselves against the legacy of 1930s photography and in opposition to the ideological impositions of wartime propaganda. As a result, Bubley's images of working-class women waiting in bars for lonely soldiers, or looking for a future beyond the confines of their boarding house existences while remaining outside the middle-class boundaries defined by capitalist consumerism, set out a pictorial foundation for working-class female identity which exists beyond the context in which the photographs were taken. Consequently, Bubley's work highlights individual self-identity, personal empowerment and self-conscious desire in working-class women which was – and still is – confined and repressed by economic disadvantage and systematic marginalization from an American society defined from a middle-class point of view.

Keywords

Bubley; photography; working class; women; American; 1940s

Class and contemplation

> Starting from her latest image, taken the summer before her death . . . I arrived, traversing three quarters of a century, at the image of a child. . . . Of course I was then losing her twice over, in her final fatigue and in her first photograph, for me the last, but it was also at this moment that everything turned around and I discovered her.
>
> (Barthes, 1984: 71)

> The house seemed empty. 'Else, Ben,' she called softly. No-one answered. Slowly, she pulled herself up and edging along the wall, pushed open the door into the front room. It lay in shadow, and out of an old enlarged photo, a very young Anna with a baby Will in her arms smiled down upon her. Her face contorted. Quickly she closed the door.
>
> (Olsen, 1980: 65)

In *Camera Lucida*, Roland Barthes follows an emotional, photographic track in an attempt to come to terms with his mother's death. In so doing, he identifies two elements which form an individual reaction to a particular image. 'Studium' connotes a general cultural response, a provocation of historical sympathy, a political commitment, or an enthusiasm for a certain event or particular set of poses. Within this what one might call a rational response, Barthes identifies the concept of 'punctum', a reaction he describes as the element 'which rises from the scene, shoots out of it like an arrow and pierces' (Barthes, 1984: 26). Punctum disturbs contemplation with an injection of irrationality, an interruption which designates the unfixable emotion of the image. Punctum signifies that element in photography which made Dorothea Lange uncomfortable with the classification of her work as factual or merely documentary: 'that magical power . . . that makes people look at it again and again and find new truths with each looking' (Ohrn, 1980: 35).

As Barthes searched through many photographs of his mother his general response was one of studium. He recognized her reproduced image but he 'missed her being' – the element of punctum (Barthes, 1984: 66). At last in one photograph, taken when she was a child in a winter garden in 1898, Barthes found what, for him, was the 'truth' of his mother's image. He does not reproduce the winter garden picture in *Camera Lucida* because the element of punctum exists only for himself, as the son of the young girl portrayed now dead. For the general readership, Barthes' mother exists only in the realm of studium where, he concludes, there can be 'no wound' (Barthes, 1984: 73).

The second passage quoted at the beginning of this article, from Tillie Olsen's novel *Yonnondio: From the Thirties*, serves as a useful illustration of Barthes' theory, widening his view beyond individual reactions to specific images into a response which identifies the relationship of photography to capitalist ideology and its prescriptive notions of class, race and gender. In the novel, Anna, a working-class mother of four children, is struggling to survive the Depression. Her existence has become engulfed by community pressures and the social demands of motherhood. For Anna, motherhood is a day-to-day tortuous struggle for survival in which any sense of self-identity has been destroyed. Her only recognition of her individuality comes when she collapses from exhaustion, and consequently has time for self-reflection. She is reminded of the demanding necessities of her role by a photograph of herself as a young woman with one of her babies. The immediacy of this image – its element of punctum – forces her to resume the arduous task of making a better life for her children, 'to which her being was bound' (Olsen, 1980: 271).

In contrast, as Barthes looks at his mother's picture, he embarks on a long, complicated reverie of self-signification. His privileged class position is made clear in opposition to Anna, whose brief sense of self is suffocated as she faces her reproduced image. For her, the act of recognition initiates a negative response. Anna's economic circumstances and the demands of motherhood engulf the drift of consciousness which should contextualize punctum into studium. Looking at the picture, she is not reminded of happier times; she does not see her child's smile or her own youth; she does not respond with nostalgia, or regret that time has taken its toll and her hopes have not been fulfilled. In this sense the photograph, and Anna's relationship to it, do not comment directly on the political and economic circumstances that have ensured her oppression. Instead, the photograph enshrines Anna's insignificance. It is a manifest denial of her need for self-expression and self-definition. As such, the photograph does not engage Anna. In her deprived material context she is repelled by the element of punctum. Within the politics of representation she does not exist. As a working-class woman she can only ever be a subject.

Working-class subjects/working-class viewers

I hesitate to draw too emphatic a conclusion from this comparison, since *Yonnondio* is a work of fiction and therefore no less problematic as a form of representation than a photograph. However, I feel it is legitimate to use Olsen's work as a starting point since it provides a rare instance of a working-class woman in the position of viewer rather than as framed subject (in this case she is both). It is the absence of this perspective which is most pertinent to the following discussion, since the majority of images taken for the United States government between 1934 and 1945 under the auspices of the Farm Security Administration (FSA) and, later, the Office of War Information (OWI), depicted working-class people and the social and economic upheavals which have come to represent their subjectivity.

The photographs taken for the FSA/OWI offer a comprehensive survey of poverty during the Depression era and the early years of the Second World War. In images made by Dorothea Lange, for example, the desperate circumstances of those portrayed were made very clear. In the liberal context of Franklin Roosevelt's New Deal, it would have been difficult for a viewer of one of the more than 200,000 FSA/OWI photographs to argue that migrant workers and tenant farmers did not require financial assistance. Public sympathy was elicited by images displayed in official reports, political surveys and photographic magazines such as *Life* and *Look*. Popular concern was subsequently voiced, and the American people who were not the focus of FSA/OWI images responded – politically, financially and with a sense of moral responsibility – to the need that was displayed before them. The central message contained in documentary photographs of this period was clear: that poverty was not an acceptable part of American society and therefore must be eased – if not eradicated – for the mutual benefit of both the subject and the viewer of FSA/OWI images. In this way government photography seemed to serve a practical purpose in the 1930s and 1940s, not only in making visible and attempting to resolve the problems of economic and social deprivation, but also in apparently bridging the psychological distance between poverty and security through the visual dynamic of documentary photography. In so doing, FDR's government could claim that even despite the factual evidence represented in the images, the economic difference between subject and viewer was secondary to the metaphoric equality evoked by the images. The construction of this ideological facade is particularly relevant to the way in which working-class identity was represented to a middle-class audience.

This iniquitous concentration away from the working-class subject suggests that FSA/OWI documentary represented a realistic portrayal of the suffering and endurance of its framed subjects, thereby justifying the need for intervention of the exact kind provided by a socially concerned, liberal government. In this scenario, subject positions are clearly defined. Working-class identity – a tenant farmer or a migrant worker, preferably with additional toothless wife and scrawny children – was depicted, in William Stott's words, as 'helpless, guiltless . . . and though helpless, yet unvanquished by the implacable wrath of nature' (Stott, 1986: 58). In this respect, the appeal to a middle-class audience was unsubtle, and was designed to arouse enough guilt and pity to induce a sufficiently charitable parting with tax dollars on the subject's behalf. At the same time, middle-class superiority – both moral and intellectual – was reconfirmed in FSA photography. The photographs do not show anger, nor do they present a threat to their intended audience. Instead, the photographs imply a simple gratitude at Christian generosity which is expressed as a naïve assurance that 'I will work for five dollars a month if I have to'. In this respect, as Maren Stange suggests, 'the documentary mode testified both to the existence of painful social facts and the reformers' expertise in ameliorating them, thus reassuring a liberal middle-class that social oversight was both its duty and its right' (Stange, 1992: XIII).

Despite having the appearance of being a vastly detailed, although simplistically conceived survey of American life in the 1930s and early 1940s, FSA/OWI photography performed a distinct purpose. The images were intended to reflect the political ethos of the New Deal, and in particular the policies of the Farm Security Administration. The ideological impetus which underscored the documentary project was promoted by Roy Stryker, the head of the historical section which controlled FSA images, who was in turn a prodigy of Rexford Tugwell who had conceived the FSA as being a way of replanning and reorganizing the agricultural economy. Both men sought to advance the idea of a technocratic, capitalist economy which would eliminate class distinctions and so create social equilibrium. 'Economic efficiency' and 'technical progress' were the watchwords of FSA policy, phrases which displayed an ideological direction that ironically undermined the agrarian mythologies captured in the photographs. This political incongruity was transformed into ideological clarity, which was made concrete in the ways FSA photographs were used to illustrate the intent, and thus the success, of FSA policies.

Since the 1930s and 1940s, the FSA/OWI file has come to represent one of the most comprehensive documents ever accumulated in American history. At the same time, however, the images have become detached from their pernicious ideological context and have been transformed into a powerfully nationalistic cultural iconography. As a result, the file itself – held in a special collection at the Library of Congress, where it might be viewed by anyone with a 'legitimate research purpose' – has effectively reconstituted historical fact into mythologized narrative. Consequently, the personalized histories of the working-class subjects portrayed have been appropriated into configurations of middle-class aestheticism, where the photographer's social purpose has been devalued and the position of the framed subject has been, in Martha Rosler's words, 'shaded over into combinations of exoticism, tourism and voyeurism, psychologism and metaphysics, trophy hunting and careerism' (Rosler, 1989: 306).

In these ways, FSA/OWI documentary photography, examined in its contemporary context and from the perspective of historic nostalgia and artistic sentimentality, has repressed working-class identity within framed subjecthood. Certainly, in passing, working-class subjectivity has been freed within the context of representation; but this politically enlightened view of a carefully contextualized image does not constitute material equality. Social and economic power are essential requirements for physical and psychological freedom which are, in turn, fundamental for developing a sense of self-recognition, creativity, political empowerment and the ability to see oneself beyond representation. A comment by John Berger, read in comparison with another passage from *Yonnondio*, illustrates this point:

> One can lie on the ground and look up at the almost infinite number of stars in the night sky, but in order to tell stories about those stars they need to be seen as constellations. The invisible lines which connect them need to be assumed.
>
> (Berger and Mohr, 1982: 284)

> 'Stars,' she began 'what are they now? Splinters off the moon I've heard it said.'
> He laughed then he told her how the stars seemed dancing . . . the Greeks who had named these stars and had found in their shapes images of what was on earth below. . . . She scarcely listened . . . only the aura of them, of timelessness, of vastness, of eternal things that had been before her and would be after her remained, and entered into her with a great hurt and longing.
>
> (Olsen, 1980: 190)

For John Berger the stars are a metaphor for the way photographs are perceived by the viewer. He speaks particularly of how images become resonant when the viewer reacts to the framed subject with his or her experience, knowledge and imagination. The viewer's position is not fixed and in dialectical interaction with the image; both become open to a plurality of meanings and interpretations. The multiplicity of possible meanings available, both to the image and to the viewer's perception, removes the need for an explanatory text which would narrow the fluidity of interpretation, and impose a repressive narrative on the photograph. This interactive process between image and viewer connotes Berger's 'invisible lines' between stars.

In his argument Berger states that the existence of the invisible lines 'must be assumed'. However, before this assumption can be made it is important to be aware of the distance between the stars; that is, the space between image and viewer which signifies a material social context. Carol Schloss has noted that 'the space between who is framed and the one who frames is a place of political action' (Schloss, 1987: 256). Making the connection is therefore an ongoing political process which, like any other in capitalist society, is constrained and manipulated by issues of class, race and gender.

Using the passage from *Yonnondio*, the inadequacy of Berger's theory is made clear. Maizie, the 6-year-old daughter of Anna, is told how individual stars are part of constellations which help explain the meaning of her identity. However, her economic circumstances and lack of education mean that she is unable to make the connection for herself. Instead, she can feel only 'the aura' of the words, and a sense of 'great hurt and longing' at her inability to articulate their meaning for herself. In this sense, Maizie's inability to recognize and understand the literal meaning of the constellations not only undermines Berger's theory, but also ironicizes Walter Benjamin's suggestion that photography is an implicitly radical artistic medium which, in its endless reproductions of images, removes the exclusive 'aura' of middle-class aestheticism through a process of mass consumption. In Maizie's case the dialectic process is not so straightforward. Her desire is not to achieve a sense of collectively formed revolutionary or proletarian consciousness, but to be able to comprehend cultural meaning for herself, as an individual from a working-class background. Thus the tragedy of Maizie's point of view in relation to the constellations is given political significance beyond Berger's and Benjamin's theories in that – as an individual working-class girl – the possibility of self-signification on her own terms cannot even enter her consciousness.

My aim in the following pages is to examine photographs by Esther Bubley, a relatively unknown photographer who worked for the historical section of the Farm Security Administration and for the Office of War Information between 1941 and 1943. My investigation begins with the view that theoretical discourses concerning self-signification and the deconstruction of ideological narratives through an intricate examination of specific contexts is unhelpful unless prefaced with an understanding of the material circumstances necessary to free oneself from the impositions of representation, and so be able to take up the position of the viewer. Furthermore, I want to place her photographs within the context of the political imperatives that begin this text; that is, the need to establish a basis of representation against which working-class women can identify themselves and consequently find the means for self-expression.

In contrast with other government-sponsored photographs of this period, Bubley constructed her images in ways that allowed her subjects to 'speak for themselves', challenging the social and material contexts in which they were placed. As such, her images portray a disconnection and isolation from society which is disturbing to the viewer, and which distorts the imposition of a conventionally middle-class narrative on to the image. Accepted points of interaction between subject and viewer are subsequently undermined and rearranged in a way that allows for the possibility of a working-class point of view. At the same time, subjecthood is not fixed within the frame since her photographs provoke a reaction which is uncomfortable, unsure and necessarily incomplete. In these ways, her photographs do not sit easily with popular and governmentally sanctioned notions of working-class female experience in official images, nor are they included within the mythologized aestheticism which has come to denote the visual history of the 1930s and early 1940s. As a result, Bubley's images are able to release working-class identity from framed subjecthood, and subsequently are able to provide a space within the image which allows for the possibility of a self-significating process begun from the subject's point of view.

The Greyhound bus trip

Esther Bubley was born in 1921 in Superior, Wisconsin, where her father was the manager of an automobile supply shop. Before becoming a photographer she studied painting at the Minneapolis School of Design. In 1940, aged 19, she moved to New York City where she got a temporary studio job with *Vogue*. In 1941 she moved to Washington, DC and began work as a microfilmer in the National Archives. Later that year she was hired as a laboratory technician by Roy Stryker (Stryker and Wood, 1973: 55).

In these respects, Esther Bubley's photographic apprenticeship was very different from that of other women who had worked for the FSA in the 1930s. Bubley's small town, lower-middle-class background pales in comparison with Dorothea Lange's intrepid documentary adventures across the country. Bubley also did not have the advantage of Marion Post Wolcott's bohemian education in Greenwich Village and Vienna. Furthermore, unlike her female predecessors, Bubley's pre-FSA photographic experience was in commercial and fashion photography rather than in socially concerned documentation, like Lange, or with photojournalism, like Post Wolcott. Bubley did not even have a driver's licence. Her photographic projects for the FSA were therefore confined to the Washington, DC area and the outskirts of Virginia. When she travelled, it was not for thousands of miles through the Southern states solo with an axe in her trunk; nor was it across the Midwest and California consumed by a vision to reconstruct a social and economic history of agricultural production in the United States. Instead, Esther Bubley travelled from Washington, DC to Memphis on an overcrowded Greyhound bus. Her view of America in the 1940s was not of an unobscured road heading west seen from the roof of her car, but looking awkwardly through the bus driver's windscreen. She stood in the aisle, precariously balanced as the bus moved along, trying not to get in the driver's way. Consequently, Bubley's vision was a little lopsided, her view not quite squarely framed.

The apparent lack of clarity in Bubley's approach appeared to be balanced by the subject matter of FSA/OWI photography in the 1940s which, according to Stryker, was decidedly less complicated than had been the case in the previous decade. As America entered the Second World War the focus of government photography shifted from images of rural poverty and Depression era economics as exemplified in FSA work, to a concentration of the nation's wealth and on the wider availability of consumer products. As a result, images made under the auspices of the Office of War Information depicted a population which appeared to be homogeneously middle class. This change in direction is highlighted by Roy Stryker's comments to Russell Lee and Arthur Rothstein:

> We must have at once: pictures of men, women and children who appear as if they really believe in the USA. Get people with a little spirit. Too many in our file now paint the US as an old people's home, and that just about everyone is too old to work and too malnourished to care much about what happens.
> (Stryker and Wood, 1973: 88)

Thematically, Bubley's photographic projects for the FSA/OWI reflected Stryker's outlook and also fitted the government's demands for a positive wartime image of mutual sacrifice and absolute faith in American victory. To this end, as well as the Greyhound bus trip which was intended to show the effectivity of gasoline and rubber rationing, Bubley photographed crowds gathered at patriotic parades to celebrate Memorial Day and cheering civil defence volunteers. She also documented high school students supporting their colleagues as they joined the armed forces, and as they studied to prepare for the bright future which was assured by the guarantee of American victory. Reflecting this patriotic purpose, Bubley's images captured soldiers and their sweethearts visiting national monuments, enshrining heterosexual love and family values alongside the symbolic constancy of American history. In the same way, Bubley's photographs of women living in boarding houses while working for the war effort also emphasized wartime reification of the family unit.

Even while their husbands, sons, brothers and fiancés were absent, visions of home and family were maintained psychologically through each woman's support for another. Unlike other FSA/OWI photographers, however, the apparently benign nature of these images was radically transformed by Bubley's ability to critically examine the narratives of wartime representation, and at the same time deconstruct the impositions of its conclusions about what officially constituted working-class identity in the early 1940s. In this respect, Bubley utilized government propaganda messages in which patriotism, nationalism and the inevitability of victory were symbolized in images of white middle-class families, usually with a perfectly domesticated, yet strongly committed woman at their centres. Bubley ironicized such portrayals by showing how those marginalized from OWI campaigns – working-class women and non-white people – interacted or, most significantly, undermined the facade of government propaganda to reveal its economic and racial prejudices. The following analysis reflects Bubley's approach. Although I have concentrated here on her images of white working-class women, my investigation could be equally applied to her photographs of African-Americans.

Bubley's Greyhound bus trip began in September 1943. The distance she covered, beginning in New York City and ending in Memphis, was reminiscent of the geographic scope of an FSA assignment. The various subjects of her images also reflected the general focus of 1930s documentary photography. She photographed women with their children, old people and people of different races. Since they were all cramped together on the bus, she also depicted the circumstances of their economic disadvantage. She photographed people performing menial labour: unloading baggage and cleaning the inside of the bus. Most obviously in line with FSA tradition, however, Bubley made images of a population on the move – dozens of people crowded together on the bus, hundreds of them pushed together in station waiting rooms, restrooms and on platforms. Her photographs of the physicality of human movement inferred a sense of visual association with the migrant populations photographed in the 1930s. This portrayal of a fundamental historical continuity between the 1940s travellers and the class and race divisions of the previous decade undermined the wartime image of optimistic renewal and national unity (Dieckmann, 1989: 55–61).

Within her visual revision of wartime imagery, Bubley represented working-class subjects – particularly women – in ways that were radically different from previous FSA photographers. For example, in one photograph she portrays a woman cleaning the interior of a bus (Figure 1). The woman's body is constricted by the tight frame of the image, and

Figure 1 'Woman cleaning the interior of a Greyhound bus.' Reproduced from the collections of the Library of Congress.

she is also physically confined by the seats on either side of the aisle. She pushes the mop in front of her as she moves towards the back of the bus. From the viewer's perspective the woman seems to be receding into the dark background, while her mop and the seats she has cleaned appear huge in comparison with her ever decreasing body size. In effect, the woman is gradually disappearing into the centre of the photograph. This sense of imminent absence is compounded in relation to Bubley's other photographs in the Greyhound bus series: of the station full of people waiting to get on the bus, or of passengers filling the bus while collectively participating in the wartime conservation of fuel and rubber. By taking this photograph in such a context, Bubley has established the essential but inevitably absent presence of a working-class woman within official narratives of wartime information. At the same time, as Bubley focuses on the light falling on the woman's arms, she highlights the way the woman pushes the mop with a certain amount of strength and purpose. There is a definite forward thrust which counterbalances her backward movement. In capturing this oppositional dynamic, Bubley has enabled the working-class woman to quietly subvert and invade the physical space occupied by the patriotic passengers, a context which was fundamental to documentary photography in the 1940s.

Bubley's subversion of OWI imperatives was extended in her radical portrayal of working-class subjects in relation to FSA tradition. Unlike photographs by Dorothea Lange or Marion Post Wolcott, who routinely photographed poverty in ways which were reassuringly other than those of the viewer, Esther Bubley used the unifying rhetorical devices of wartime information ironically to show the personalized proximity of racial injustice and economic inequity to every individual American. Thus oppression and injustice in Bubley's Greyhound bus images are not visibly received as exclusive 'whites only' signposts or as depictions of 'the other side of the tracks', but as being fundamentally intrinsic to the actual bodies, psychological sensibilities and intimate desires of both the working-class subject and the middle-class viewer.

The Sea Grill bar

Bubley used the enclosed space of the Greyhound bus to highlight the ways in which white, middle-class – particularly female – bodies were closely guarded, politically protected spaces in American culture. This point was extended within the context of OWI images since white, middle-class female identity became symbolic of the war's purpose. Men fought to protect America for their wives, mothers and daughters, while women remained at home, loyal and chaste, so that the men could be welcomed home in a satisfying fashion. To this end punitive legislation was enacted in order to reinforce this suggestively gendered, economically and racially specific rhetoric.

Karen Anderson has noted that a 'renewed vigilance on female sexual conduct' became an integral part of official information in the 1940s (Anderson, 1981: 140). Her study concentrates on a wartime housing project in Seattle, where women were routinely arrested for prostitution under the auspices of the Social Protection Division of the Office of Community War Services. The division led a campaign to search for 'incipient and confirmed sex delinquents' (Anderson, 1981: 104). Their powers extended to a broad definition of sexual misconduct applying only to women, which included 'promiscuity: i.e. sexual activity without sincere emotional content; or endangering moral safety or health: i.e. frequenting bars, loitering etc., without a male escort' (Anderson,

1981: 105). The penalties for such crimes included mandatory testing for sexually transmitted diseases and a jail sentence while results were awaited, which in some cases could be up to five days. Anderson concludes that as a result, between 1940 and 1944, there was a 95 per cent increase in women charged with 'moral violations', and in Seattle alone three hundred women were detained every month.

There is a clear class bias in such moral judgements. The sentences given to women arrested for moral delinquency required them to 'work, live a clean and temperate life, keep good company, and stay away from undesirable places' (Anderson, 1981: 107). The middle-class standards which underscore such statements are emphasized in Anderson's study, when one notes that the threat of moral decline in Seattle was blamed on the influx of migrant workers who lived in poverty-stricken war housing projects. A comment made by the Police Chief in a Seattle newspaper makes this point clear: 'The area is flooded with war working families who have come here from the Midwest. Parents are busy working and the kids run wild. The young fellows are making too much money' (Anderson, 1981: 97). His statement was compounded in an editorial which expressed the trepidation of the middle-class suburb of Denton towards the housing project, which they perceived as being a veritable hotbed of moral decline and misbehaviour: 'The young people [in the housing project] had access to liquor and throw promiscuous parties which would only admit girls if they had sex with all the men' (Anderson, 1981: 10).

Such fears were fuelled by an underlying need for established middle-class communities to maintain a psychological class hierarchy within a city which was supposed to be united by the war effort. The legislative effect of such middle-class fears ensured the victimization of working-class people – especially women – under the government's morality police. One might presume that it was not only working-class women who took advantage of their husbands' absences, yet it was the working-class housing projects that were most vigorously policed and it was working-class women who were left out of the loyal, hardworking, efficient and capable image of women during the war. Thus officially morally reprehensible female sexual expression was effectively transposed on to the bodies of working-class women.

Reflecting this process, in March 1943 Esther Bubley took a series of photographs at The Sea Grill, a restaurant bar in Washington, DC. She made portraits of the barman and the waitresses as well as the many customers – soldiers and civilians – but she focused on one woman in particular. The young woman is first photographed alone,

Figure 2 'Girl sitting alone in the Sea Grill waiting for a pickup.' Reproduced from the collections of the Library of Congress.

and then later laughing and drinking with two soldiers. The first photograph of the woman on her own is accompanied by a caption, selected by Bubley from the young woman's own words:

> I come here pretty often, sometimes alone, mostly with another girl, we drink beer, and talk, and of course we keep our eyes open. You'd be surprised at how often nice lonesome soldiers ask Sue, the waitress, to introduce them to us.
>
> (Fisher, 1987: 95)

Bubley also added the additional caption, 'Girl sitting alone in the Sea Grill waiting for a pickup' (Figure 2). The viewer is not given a sense of the woman's age, marital status, background or moral standards, but from her own words it is at least clear that she intends to meet a soldier as she does on frequent nights, and ease his loneliness by showing him a good time. Whatever the might imply sexually, the woman is certainly making herself available for the attention of 'nice lonesome soldiers'.

In terms of government sponsored representation then, this woman is on the edge of what was defined as social acceptability. Indeed, in certain states she would have broken laws designed to maintain the moral unity of American family life. As such, even if her presence in the Sea Grill bar was not illegal in the District of Columbia, it was certainly made illegitimate by the rhetoric of government information. Nevertheless, the way that Bubley has constructed the photograph detracts from any suggestion of seediness or moral suspicion. The atmosphere is certainly moody, but not in any way disturbing. Light falls on the woman's face, making her seem beautiful, almost fragile. This feeling is enhanced by her look away from the camera, perhaps in an expression of self-possession, but also of self-protection. Her legs are crossed and her arms folded in front of her, placing her beyond the reach of the camera's gaze – and consequently the viewer's moral judgement. Her apparent obliviousness is compounded when one notes that there is a man's face behind the woman, looking through the window from the street, through the blinds covering the window, over the woman's head and, with one eye, apparently noticing and confronting the camera. Even from such a distance, the man seems to be more aware of being looked at than the woman. This contrast is ironic since from her stated intention the viewer might assume that the woman wants to be looked at, that she has put herself on display, and that she consequently deserves whatever action or judgement such a display might invite. Conversely, in the construction and lighting of the photograph, Bubley has undercut the power of the viewer's gaze and as a result has revealed the pejorative class bias of official representation. To this end, Bubley has used her training in fine art and commercial photography to complicate the woman's self-identity beyond predesignated social and political meaning.

Bubley's perspective is clearly evocative of Edward Hopper's painting 'Automat' (1927). There is the same sense of disaffection and social detachment. The woman is waiting alone in the corner of the booth, while the rest of the seating area takes up almost one-third of the frame. The distance between her handbag and crumpled napkin leaves an available space for somebody, but the sense of isolation is so profound that one gets the feeling that the absence will never be filled. Indeed, when the photograph is interpreted using the Hopperesque visual language evoked by Bubley, the fleeting attachments made by this woman each night become infused with a sense of pathos and nihilism. In contrast to 1930s applications of painting to documentary photography, where a working-class subject's identity was submerged beneath the impositions of artistic misrepresentation, Bubley has used Hopper's work to reveal an emotional depth to this woman which the viewer might otherwise refuse. Furthermore, by covering the image with the metaphysical aura of a painting, Bubley has enabled the woman – who is real – to play the part of one of Hopper's female subjects. Consequently, her real identity is never exposed to the viewer.

The conscious sense of unreality and disguise in this photograph is extended further by Bubley. Although the woman's face is brightly lit, she is evidently sitting among shadows. This, together with her pose, her appearance and the way she holds her cigarette, is consistent with the conventions of a film noir heroine. In this guise, the woman is able to transgress social codes and acceptable spaces that would have otherwise placed her in politicized sexual jeopardy. Following the narrative progress of the filmic language her appearance evokes, she is placed beyond the reach of middle-class wartime mythology. Like most of Bubley's photographic subjects, she can exist between repressive wartime narratives and beyond the conventions of documentary photography.

The boarding house

Esther Bubley explores the radical space negotiated in the construction of the Sea Grill bar photograph further in a series of images taken at Arlington farms, a residence for women who worked for the US government, and at a boarding house in Washington, DC. The majority of the women living in boarding houses and residence halls were lower middle-class and working-class women who had come to the city in search of well-paid clerical jobs, as well as for excitement and romance only dreamed of in their rural and midwestern homes. Often they would be disappointed and return home. Otherwise they would stay, struggling to survive depressed living conditions and exploitative work situations.

Like migrant families in FSA images of the 1930s, these women formed a constant stream of expendable labour. Unlike their counterparts of the previous decade, however, officially sponsored representations showed these women as aspiring to an appearance of middle-class sophistication which, in reality, proved very difficult to maintain. In Bubley's boarding house images, the process through which working-class identity was constructed in this context is explored. More significant however is her portrayal of the way these women lived beyond middle-class conventions of acceptability and appearance, and created their own individualized senses of identity and personal self-expression.

In the first instance, Bubley was acutely aware that in the 1940s femininity was portrayed as being fundamentally acquisitive and thus constitutive of material privilege. An individual woman had to be able to 'buy' a suitably middle-class appearance in order to be considered socially

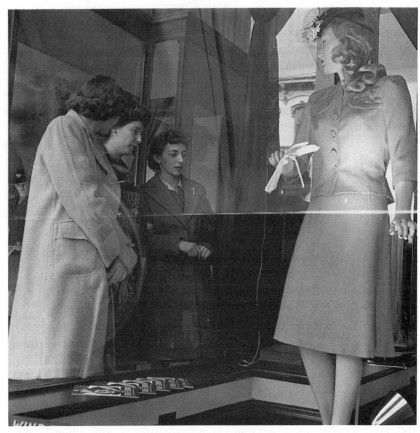

Figure 3 'Girls window shopping, Washington, DC, December 1943.'
Reproduced from the collections of the Library of Congress.

acceptable. In 1940s systems of representation, this was not simply a matter of accepting the vestiges of bourgeois snobbery, but of being able to participate fully in an economic, social and political context in which middle-class values, beliefs and appearances were institutionalized and disseminated by the government.

The connection between economic exclusion and the politicization of middle-class appearance is made clear in one image, 'Girls window shopping, Washington, DC, December 1943' (Figure 3). In this photograph, three young women are gathered around a shop window looking at clothes displayed on a female mannequin. Significantly, they are physically separated from the objects of their collective desire by a glass barrier. Since they do not have the means which would allow them entry, Bubley has established an economic division in this photograph. From this position, she has also constructed an element of social hierarchy between the consumer items on display in the window and the three women who remain outside. The mannequin is positioned close to the foreground of the frame, making 'her' appear much larger than the real women, who stand to the left of the photograph's centre. Almost two-thirds of the frame is taken up by the window display. Moreover, the mannequin's left arm is poised as if to move towards the three women. In contrast, the women stand close together, almost huddled, their hands crossed in front of themselves, eyes lowered without meeting the gaze frozen on the mannequin. This opposition endows the well-dressed mannequin with more physical space, more sense of movement, more height, even more self-possession than the real women. What is more, the mannequin is better groomed, more attractively made up, and is dressed with more sophistication than the three women outside. The mannequin represents the manifestation of the middle-class appearance desired by the women, but because of their economic position they are marginalized from the material and social power over which the mannequin presides.

None the less, because Bubley has chosen to portray economic exclusion in the guise of a store mannequin, she is able to show the artificiality of middle-class identity. It is this sense of insubstantiality which allows for the possibility of imitation, infiltration and possible subversion by the economically underprivileged women. Reflecting this possibility, it is not clear whether Bubley has taken the photograph from inside or outside the shop window. The reflection from the glass cuts across the viewer's perspective and places the women in the artificial space occupied by the mannequin. From this point of view, the real women are empowered in relation to the mannequin; they now possess the ability to deceive the viewer's gaze. It is this power – to defy the viewer and retain a sense of self-identity despite ideologically inscribed notions of class position and aspiration – that is most radical and important in Bubley's boarding house images. Her approach removes her subjects from the visual expectations of traditional documentary photography and also from the narrative process of wartime imagery and politics. In so doing, Bubley captures the self-identified subjective processes of the boarding house women, and simultaneously complicates the visual connection between the viewer and the depicted subject. The women in Bubley's photographs construct their own personal narratives, despite their economic disadvantages, in such a way that their subjecthood excludes the middle-class viewer. The complexity of this construction is made clear in one image, an apparently simple portrait of a young woman looking out of her window, staring at a large house across the street (Figure 4). The photograph is captioned 'Boarders often speculate on the identity of the

Figure 4 'Boarders often speculate on the identity of the owner of the house across the street. They like to think it belongs to the president of a South American steamship line.' Reproduced from the collections of the Library of Congress.

owner of the house across the street. They like to think it belongs to the president of a South American steamship line'.

In this photograph, the woman who is the subject of the image is portrayed in silhouette to the far right of her frame. Only her head and arms are visible to the viewer. To the left of the picture there are a few articles – a lamp, a bottle of water and a newspaper – which presumably belong to the woman. At the top left- and right-hand corners of the photograph there are some lacy curtains. But the central focus of the image is the large house outside the window, surrounded by trees and a manicured lawn. The house is certainly huge, with a stone pillar entrance and a sweeping driveway with a shiny black car parked outside. The viewer makes the connection between the caption of the photograph and the house which is the central focus. This point is vital. What Bubley has photographed is not the woman, or her room, or the big house with the car outside it, but the daydreamed thoughts of the woman looking out of the window, or at least Bubley's imaginings of what the woman's thoughts might be. In either case, Bubley has given a mental process physical shape and depicted the self-consciousness of the woman. Certainly, the caption offers the viewer some idea about what the woman is thinking, but Bubley's construction is more complicated than that. The viewer is provided with the material evidence of the woman's speculation about the big house, but the direction of the gaze leads beyond the house, and follows the road out of the frame of the image. This sense of unfixable movement is compounded by the car which, from the viewer's perspective, is only half visible through the trees, but which, to the woman, must be unobscured. The train of reverie is accelerated in equation with the car; consequently along with it, the woman's self-conscious individuality is allowed to exist beyond the frame of the image.

In her book *Let Us Now Praise Famous Women*, Andrea Fisher labelled the element of psychological dynamism in Bubley's work 'the drift of reverie' (Fisher, 1987: 15). I feel this analysis to be unconscious of the radical materiality of Bubley's photographs, which I have tried to convey in my analysis. In comparison with other FSA and OWI photographers, Bubley was uniquely able to represent economically oppressed people in ways that are potentially liberating and implicitly revolutionary. In the 1940s, she was able to work between the official images of narratives of wartime representation. In so doing, she exposed the class and race biases which were central to the rhetorical success of government-sponsored information. At the same time, she was able to create a space in her photographs for the self-identified presence of her subjects – but she did not expose them. She allowed them to create their own subjecthood, to disguise themselves, to hide, to confuse the viewer. Most significantly, however, the people she portrayed in her images do not remain within the frame. They are presented in a way that demands a dialectical process of narrative construction between subject and viewer from *the subject's point of view*. As a result, Bubley radically complicated not only what it meant to be the subject of a documentary photograph, but also what it meant politically, socially and subjectively to be a working-class woman in the 1940s – and beyond.

Note

Jacqueline Ellis completed her Ph.D. in American Studies at the University of Hull. She is now living in the United States where she is hoping to publish her book, *Silent Witnesses: Representations of Working-class Women in America 1933–1945*.

References

ANDERSON, Karen (1981) *Wartime Women: Sex Roles, Family Relations and the Status of Women During World War Two* Westport, CT: Greenwood Press.
BARTHES, Roland (1984) *Camera Lucida* London: Flamingo.
BERGER, John and MOHR, Jean (1982) *Another Way of Telling* New York: Pantheon.
BOLTON, Richard (1989) editor, *The Contest of Meaning: Critical Histories of Photography* Cambridge, MA: MIT Press.
DIECKMANN, Katherine (1989) 'A nation of zombies: government files contain the extraordinary unpublished photographs that Esther Bubley took on one long bus ride across America' in *Art in America* (November 1989).
FISHER, Andrea (1987) *Let Us Now Praise Famous Women: Women Photographers for the US Government 1935 to 1945* London: Pandora.
OHRN, Karin Becker (1980) *Dorothea Lange and the Documentary Tradition* Baton Rouge: Louisiana State University Press.
OLSEN, Tillie (1980) *Yonnondio: from the Thirties* London: Virago.
ROSLER, Martha (1989) 'in, around and afterthoughts (on documentary photography)' in **Bolton**, editor.
SCHLOSS, Carol (1987) *In Visible Light: Photography and the American Writer 1840–1940* New York: Oxford University Press.
STANGE, Maren (1992) *Symbols of Ideal Life: Social Documentary Photography in America* New York: Cambridge University Press.
STOTT, William (1986) *Documentary Expression and Thirties America* Austin: University of Texas Press.
STRYKER, Roy and WOOD, Nancy (1973) *In This Proud Land: America 1935–1943, as seen in the FSA Photographs* New York: New York Graphic Society.

Between Identification and Desire:
Rereading *Rebecca*

Janet Harbord

> One needs to read the drama of the Symbolic, of desire, of the institution of sexual difference as a self-supporting signifying economy that wields power in the marking off of what can and cannot be thought within the terms of cultural intelligibility. *Mobilizing the distinction between what is 'before' and what is 'during' culture is one way to foreclose cultural possibilities from the start.*
>
> (Judith Butler, 1990: 78, my emphasis)

> We can never go back again, that much is certain. The past is still too close to us.
>
> (Du Maurier, 1938: 8)

Both psychoanalysis and conventional romance narratives are discourses that depend on, and reproduce, a dialectic of past and present; reading the present against the past produces implicitly a notion of the temporal as advancement. For each discourse, to move in time is to progress from a state of flux to a state of stability. What is 'before', as Butler notes above in relation to psychoanalysis, is what is discarded; subsequently that which is delegitimized through narratives of Oedipalization and romance. The present is established as 'real' only in relation to a past that has been othered, reworked and reconfigured to give eminence to the present of identity. In psychoanalysis the theory of the psychic life of the individual is dependent on this linear perspective, the trajectory from the undifferentiated pre-Oedipal realm to the notion of self (Freud), from the pre-linguistic to the subject in language (Lacan). Yet in neither psychoanalysis nor romance fiction is the past successfully contained, closed off, hermetically sealed. The past returns to haunt, to ghost the present and disturb the familiarity of 'home'. My interest here is in the paradox that while teleological mapping characterizes the form and intelligibility of each of these narratives, the appeal of returning and repetition offers a form of pleasure that is never fully contained. In *Rebecca*, despite the narrator's profession to the contrary, 'we' are continually going back, returning, because the appeal of what is prohibited is often stronger than the appeal of the 'present' limits of conformity.

In this article recent debates in queer theory concerning subjectivity and reading, sex and gender, are used to read the genre of romance fiction, focusing in particular on Du Maurier's *Rebecca* as an exemplary text of returning. My argument is that although narrative structures, particularly of romance, work to contain possibilities normatively, such as sexual object choice, in order for this to appear precisely as both choice and destiny necessitates the textual exploration of other possibilities. In romance fiction the most substantial part of the text is concerned with other potential outcomes on the way to closure (heterosexuality, marriage), and the retrospective ordering of events as *the* legitimate path through these murky woods is often the final moment of clarification and enlightenment. The pleasures of the meandering path are the concerns of romance fiction. Certainly in *Rebecca*, the text is dominated by the girl's fascination with, and arguably desire for the ghostly image of Rebecca, to be repressed by the narrative mechanism only with some difficulty (Light, 1984). The appeal of the genre then is in part the pleasure of transgression on the way to conformity; (the fantasy of) memory above presence.

In what might seem like an unlikely coupling, I want to argue that recent work in queer theory (Butler, 1990; Sedgwick, 1990) which problematizes the Oedipal configuration of identification and desire shares certain parallels with romance fiction. The axes of identification (with the same sex) and desire (for the opposite sex) are in romance fiction significantly imbricated, allowing the reader a vicarious blurring of textual pleasures. The excesses and contradictions that condition gender and sexuality surface here where the reader is invited to fantasize the spectacle of femininity (in this case Rebecca) in an indistinct tension of desire for and identification with her. While the narrative structure of romance may be seen to ultimately reproduce the Oedipal incest taboo and the demands of gender identity, it is also (and particularly in *Rebecca*) a regulation of same-sex desire. According to Butler's reordering of the narrative sequence, the injunction against same-sex desire precedes the prohibitions of incest:

> Because identifications substitute for object relations, and identifications are the consequence of loss, gender identification is a kind of melancholia in which the sex of the prohibited object is internalised as a prohibition. . . . The resolution of the Oedipal complex affects gender identification through not only the incest taboo, but, prior to that, the taboo against homosexuality.
>
> (Butler, 1990: 63)

To reconfigure romance within these terms as the playing out of a taboo of same-sex desire would suggest that the genre is open to transgressive readings outside/against the strictly normative heterosexual matrix, even if the narrative works ultimately (and at times unconvincingly) to contain and close these possibilities. This is not to make claims for the 'meaning' of a text/genre, but to suggest reading positions that are mobilized by the text, various roles for readers to take up, renounce, perform. And if romance reading is about repetition, it is because neither the text nor Oedipalization can fix or make concrete subjectivity in time. Mary Ann Doane states (in a more negative context): 'The compulsion to repeat, based on forgetting, is a loss of temporal differentiation, the collapse of the past onto the present', but this repetition might be viewed here as the failure of normative teleological structures to separate our sexual identity into a differentiated past and present (Doane, 1991: 95). A wilful forgetting leads the return, and the whole process of remembering, which is also a reconfiguring, begins again.

Readers of romance

The postscript to Alison Light's article, '"Returning to Manderley" romance fiction, female sexuality and class', offers this rationale of romance reading, that women are 'offered unique opportunities for reader-power, for an imaginary control of the uncontrollable in the fiction of romance', and again that 'within the realities of women's lives, they may well be transgressive . . . a forbidden pleasure' (Light, 1984). Since this article has been published a body of work has developed around 'women's genres', extending from romance fiction to television soap operas and melodrama films (Ang, 1985; Geraghty, 1991; Gledhill, 1987; Radway, 1987). Methodological shifts are discernible in this debate about locating 'meaning' in an interdisciplinary range of texts, moving from an English literary investigation of textual meaning, through semiotics, to a more sociologically influenced ethnographic account of audience/reader response. The antagonisms between feminism and Marxism – of why women read 'ideologically reactionary' material, and develop such 'compulsive' reading habits – and pleasure, have been superseded by a concern with differences in readings. This has meant locating readers within historic, geographic and cultural contexts, and cross-referencing this material with the categories of ethnicity, sexuality, age and other such factors (Radway, 1984; Seiter *et al.*, 1989). The result, particularly in television studies, has been the production of a range of projects on diverse and specific audiences, testimony perhaps to the reduced horizons of knowledge in postmodern times. I want to suggest in place of a return to 'real' audiences an analysis of a dialectic of textual possibilities and reader roles, spaces that are open to readers. The notion of readers as reflexive about their own roles and practices suggests then a level of performance in textual engagement.

The reading of *Rebecca* that follows draws on this work, furthering investigations into diverse readings of what has become a 'classic' text, posing the question of what this text, and possibly other romance fiction, might offer a queer (oppositionally situated) reader. In a further movement I want to turn this debate around, and ask how *Rebecca* might reframe some of the suppositions around desire and identification prevalent in western culture. Indeed, what these two debates (reading subjects and sexual identity) have in common is the interrogation of the limits of identification and desire, and an interrogation of the relation between gender and sexuality.

The theorization of queer reading positions has perhaps primarily taken place in relation to visual culture. The subject/spectator debate that emerged in the last decade in the wake of Laura Mulvey's influential article (Mulvey, 1975) produced a number of essays on lesbian readings of film, notably Jackie Stacey's 'Desperately seeking difference' (Stacey, 1987). Stacey argued against Mulvey's deterministic account of gendered viewing, the most problematic notion being the spectator's objectification of the female character via a relay of looks, channelled through the male protagonist. The female spectator within Mulvey's model is implicated in a system which reproduces sexual difference visually, and demands a form of masochism in the simultaneous objectification of and identification with the female character. Stacey argues against this, on the grounds that gendered reading positions are neither so unified nor totalized, either as they are produced by the text or taken up by the spectator; hence the possibility of cross-gender identification, and a more flexible notion of cinematic pleasure.

The debate on cinematic identification becomes problematic in two ways. First, the triadic relation between the cinematic apparatus, the experience of spectating and psychic processes remains untheorized, grouped as a series of parallels around a scopic mechanism. It is tempting to further the series of parallels and to argue that female spectators, like the female child of Freud's Oedipal scenario, are caught within a masculine framework of desire. Within this model the contortions necessary for the female subject to retain a heterosexual position both within the normative familial structure and as a film spectator are substantial. Given the spectacle of femininity as desirable image, the position as female subject/ spectator is one of renouncing desire in order to retain the legitimized position of heterosexuality with little in return. At the heart of both accounts (of psychic development and spectatorship) then is the cultural difficulty of heterosexuality for the female subject, and a significant paring down of possibilities. The second problem with this theory of spectatorship is that it totalizes the cinematic apparatus as effective in its operation. The notion of 'reading against the grain' is the only option available within this framework, and yet ironically this concept, as Doane points out, consolidates the totality of the mechanism: 'Such a definition of resistance is merely another acknowledgment of the totalizing aspect of the apparatus' (Doane, 1991: 79).

Film theory also colludes with the psychoanalytic notion of same-sex desire as gender inversion, not as a performative sliding across the categories but as a masochistic practice imposed by the institution of cinema. In Mulvey's account, for the female spectator to desire the image of femininity on screen is either to relate narcissistically, or to take up a male desiring position. Thus, same-sex desire becomes mapped on to the binary of a heterosexual gender inversion, a reading that disregards the potentially destabilizing effect of cross-gender identification. To contain the possibilities of spectating within this normative framework, that same-sex desire suggests gender inversion at a literal level, returns the debate to Freud and the notion of penis envy. Significantly it forecloses the possibility of opening out the fictionality of all gender identity (Butler, 1990; Sedgwick, 1990).

What is also at stake here is the argument of cultural effectiveness: either culture is a complicit site in the reproduction of hierarchized social relations or it is a less determined space of possible resistance, antagonism and appropriation of meaning. I am arguing that literary texts certainly offer ways of interpolating subjects, placing subjects and bringing them into being provisionally through an imaginary relation. But the term 'imaginary' retains a level of ambiguity that defies determinism. Identification is neither as fixed and static as film theory has presented it, nor necessarily as implicated in determining such a particular configuration of gender/sex roles for spectators/readers. Rather, identification as a process offers a series of possible roles for the reader. While Alison Light has argued for the pleasure of romance as a fantasy of class, gender and heterosexuality, I would suggest that the reading of romance can also be a process of taking up and renouncing positions *on the road to* heterosexuality, rather than the destination itself. I want to suggest that transgressive desire is ostensibly organized culturally within a sequence of moves towards a 'final goal', but that in romance fiction, and culture generally, there remains an ambivalence that this staging of desire does not fully alleviate. The strength of desire generated along this trajectory conditions the difficulty of its repression; same-sex desire cannot be laid to rest. The appeal of this transgression is evidenced outside of romance, for example, in fan cultures where identification and desire are inexplicably bound together. Heterosexuality closes uncomfortably and perhaps without conviction on these narratives, often with a compulsion to return to the beginning again.

'Being above all that': Danny's story

Mary Ann Doane, in 'Remembering women', writes:

> In psychoanalysis, the past is aggressive – it returns, it haunts, it sometimes dominates the present. In historiography, the past is static, inert – qualities which make it, in effect, more knowable.
>
> (Doane, 1991: 91)

In film noir the past that returns is the first, an aggressive disruptive past that has the power to reach into and affect the present, or one which must be repressed. *Rebecca*, and indeed many historical romance novels, evokes this same psychoanalytic sense of the past which cannot, like historiography, be exposed, known, understood. It is a past that is glimpsed, made intangible yet desirable, present yet invisible. The figure of the ghost in literary texts represents this paradox of the effectiveness of the past on the present in terms of a trope, one which is suggested in *Rebecca* but not fully announced. The memory of Rebecca certainly haunts the characters and dominates the text as a sort of absent centre of desire, the imaginary lack. Recalled through others' memories, never in flashback as perceptual evidence, Rebecca is intimately tied to the fictionality of desire, always in the process of construction for the reader, recalled 'through the eyes' of a number of characters.

The textual strategy of *Rebecca* demands that the reader collude with characters in their fascination with the past, and Rebecca. 'We' too are invited to measure the girl's ineptitude, plainness, lack of sophistication against Rebecca's conventionally heroic beauty, brains and breeding. Indeed, the emphasis on class and ethnicity hint at a sort of racial superiority where English whiteness has a luminosity that is in part transcendental, surviving the grave, somewhere between angel and ghost. Descriptions of her regulate the narrative whether the speaker is male or female, 'that cloud of dark hair against the very white skin . . . she was very beautiful', and 'I suppose she was the most beautiful creature I ever saw in my life', in a hyperbolic emphasis on physicality.

Above all, the most passionate evocations of Rebecca come from Mrs Danvers (Rebecca's pet name for her an androgynous 'Danny'), who recounts conversations, routines, habits, sayings, gestures, every detail of her mistress's physical presence:

> 'You would forget her height, until she stood beside you. She was every bit as tall as me. But lying there in bed she looked quite a slip of a thing, with her mass of dark hair, standing out from her face like a halo.'

> 'I would always know when she had been before me in a room. There would be a little whiff of her scent in the room.'

> 'That quick, light footstep. I could not mistake it anywhere. And in the minstrel's gallery above the hall. I've seen her leaning there, in the evenings in the old days, looking down at the hall below and calling to the dogs.'

Her obsessive recall of Rebecca is matched by an obsessive preservation of her rooms. In scenes reminiscent of Miss Haversham, time stands still when love is lost, a sort of taxidermy of memory. From Danny we hear of a Rebecca who rebelled against the conventions of an aristocratic femininity; a woman who rode horses sadistically and sailed alone, who cut her hair short, who wore trousers and shirts, who travelled to London by herself, had her own set of friends separate from her husband and who on occasion slept away from her husband: 'Rebecca slashing at her horse; Rebecca seizing life with two hands.' Just as Rebecca's presence dominates Manderley after her death, so it dominates the narrative without making an appearance.

The emphasis on clothes, on Rebecca's wardrobe and her last worn garments, places an emphasis on costume and appearance, which sets up a binary between artifice and authenticity. This set of oppositional values ultimately works to condemn Rebecca in the course of the narrative, when the 'true' Rebecca is revealed as a manipulator of truth, a deceiver. What is interesting about this, and perhaps part of the contemporary appeal of the text, is Rebecca's masquerade of femininity, the flaunting of the theatricality of gender identity. Rebecca has learned through her own social ascent how femininity is constructed in all its class manifestations; therefore this knowledge is used by her. Marriage is a farce, a game: 'they'll say we are the luckiest, happiest, handsomest couple in all England. What a leg-pull, Max!' At the beginning of the marriage, we learn, the bargain is struck: the pretence of respectable married life in exchange for discreet sexual freedom. Yet Rebecca does not simply invert a binary of virgin/whore; she refuses the terms of this restriction, to be contained by the structure. Later in the narrative we learn from Danny that 'She despised all men. She was above all that', and significantly:

> 'Love-making was a game to her, only a game. She told me so. She did it because it made her laugh. . . . She laughed at you as she did all the rest. I've known her come back and sit upstairs in her bed and rock with laughter at the whole lot of you.'

But what characterizes Rebecca is fluidity, the ability to shift between subject positions and across social and cultural spaces, to transform herself. What Rebecca is ultimately condemned for within the text is also what makes her appealing: her transgression of the categories of class, gender and sexuality.

While this artifice is tendered on one level as an inauthenticity (surface trickery), in terms of sexual relations the text offers no alternative, no 'real' sexual relation to supplant the only eroticism in the text. The marriage between Max de Winter and the girl is overly paternal. Representations of passion and erotic charge are confined to Rebecca who, problematically for the narrative in terms of gender, activates and inspires sexual interest. The failure to construct a heterosexuality that is passionate leaves open the interpretations of the paradigm of sexuality/gender. Masculinity has no resistance to an active desiring femininity, it must succumb and therefore lose power. The result then is a struggle to the death; heterosexual eroticism ends in a battle of control. Desiring femininities are presented in the text as able to sustain the relation, for both recognize the artifice of the game; it is this state of 'play' that is the source of erotic charge within the text. What we might tentatively conclude against the grain of romance convention is that *Rebecca* offers a vision of eroticism sustainable only for and between women.

The girl in part learns this as her sexual and social awakening, and then comes to reject it, accepting the safety of Max's asexual male power (and social standing) to the erotic charge that (the memory of) Rebecca represents. However, the text presents this dilemma in a somewhat skewed way, but one which tells us much, I would argue, about the cultural construction of sexuality. The question thus becomes, does the girl want to be like Rebecca (which she clearly is not) or does she desire her? The struggle around Rebecca for the girl is about her own social inferiority, but also about her resistance/willingness to fantasize (the memory of) Rebecca. Certainly Rebecca quickly comes to dominate her thoughts, even to the extent that, like Danny, she can imagine her presence:

In a minute, Rebecca herself would come back into the room, sit down before the looking-glass at her dressing-table, humming a tune, reach for a comb and run it through her hair. If she sat there I should see her reflection in the glass and she should see me, standing like this by the door. Nothing happened.

What I want to suggest is that in *Rebecca* this moment of ambiguity is played out – is it sexual desire for or identification with? – in terms of a desire that has been courted but must be repressed. Desire for the same sex must, both in terms of the text and of culture generally, be integrated and reinterpreted; integrated either in terms of a teleological mapping (deviant desire as a negative stage of ambiguity located in adolescence), or reinterpreted as an issue of positive identification (role models). This moment of ambiguity is less clear than is indicated and contained only retrospectively, both in terms of *Rebecca* where the narrative must convolute to represent Rebecca as corrupt, and as a cultural process. The following section briefly turns to psychoanalysis to unpack more fully the process of desire and identification as it is constructed culturally.

Mapping the perverse

In an article 'Freud and his uses: psychoanalysis and gay theory', John Fletcher examines the potential use of psychoanalysis as a mode of explication for gay studies (Fletcher, 1989). While registering the negative impact of psychoanalysis for gay subjects as it has been institutionalized, Fletcher indicates the ways in which psychoanalytic theory can be appropriated by gay theory for a more radical application. The starting point is the concept of perversity itself, Freud's perverse drive. Fletcher makes the point (also made elsewhere) that the translation of the words 'instinkt' and 'trieb' elides the meaning of each, producing the singular English term 'instinct', with its suggestion of biological destiny. The distinction between 'instinkt' and 'trieb' is crucial, for it reverses this sense of biological determinism; 'instinkt', Fletcher notes, refers to pre-given hereditary behavioural reflexes, tied to a set of needs and objects, for example, hunger and food. 'Trieb' by contrast refers to a frontier between the body and the mind, in other words, the way in which the mind conceptualizes the body, 'a set of physical representations'. The significance of this for Fletcher is that sexuality as a drive is always psychosexuality, a process that constructs images of the body and creates needs around it, as opposed to an innate sexual need.

The sexual drive or 'trieb' also has a pressure, an aim, an object and a source, but each is a psychosexual representation dependent on the contingent relation between the somatic and the mental. The aim of the sexual drive might be formulated as the pleasurable release of tension which will be played out through a series of acts and in relation to a range of objects. The 'core sights', as Fletcher calls them, are mouth, anus, urethra, as 'excitable breaks or turnings within the body'. Sexuality as it emerges then perverts the order of biological need and enters a semiotic network of signifiers detached from 'needs', which are endlessly displaced and substituted. The effect, as Fletcher notes, is a concept of sexuality as a highly mobile field of shifting signs and mental representations.

Significantly here, sexuality as it emerges does not depend on a distinction between desire and identification. In fact, the development of the ego depends on the imaginary incorporation of the breast, a connection with the maternal that fails to distinguish between the two identities. In Lacanian terms, the child supplements and fulfils the maternal desire, is the phallic object, and in turn the maternal function fulfils the infant's needs. There is no distinction between being and having, identification and desire. This emerges only in the transformation imposed by the Oedipal complex which forces a recognition of identity through separation. The story here is a familiar one, with its prohibition of incest and its positioning of the subject along the sharply defined lines of sexual difference. What is important is not only that the possibilities of sexual pleasure are significantly pared down, but also that they are channelled into a structure that endorses sexual identity through a rigid paradigm of identification. The Oedipal taboo demands that access to the mother be regulated via the paternal, in other words through identification with the father. Similarly, any libidinal investment for the female child necessitates an identification with the mother; thus gender emerges not only as social identity but also sexual definition. The significance of the Oedipal law is not only the prohibition of access to phallic power, as has been the focus of much feminist debate, but also the prohibition, 'You cannot be what you desire; you cannot desire what you wish to be' (Fletcher, 1989: 101).

The complex ways in which desire intersects with identification, or refusals of identification that are equally significant, have been taken up perhaps most interestingly in the work of Gayle Rubin, Eve Sedgwick and Judith Butler. Here the psychoanalytic narrative becomes fully problematized by what has become known as queer theory, but problematized without being superseded. In 'Axiomatic', Sedgwick renders the twin axes of identification and desire obsolete in a critical gesture towards the multiple social, historical and political differences that differentiate us from each other. In addition, she insists on our own difference within ourselves, our own others that are also internalized. In a similar way Butler's essay 'Phantasmatic Identification' explodes the notion of identification as a discrete process or event. In her terms it is closer to an imaginary staging that never achieves a stability in direction or object:

> When can we say with confidence that an identification has happened? Significantly, it never can be said to have taken place; identification does not belong to the world of events . . . [but] is the phantasmatic staging of the event.
>
> (Butler, 1993: 105)

Yet psychoanalysis remains important for queer theory in many ways, even, or especially, as a narrative that is disputed, rewritten and deconstructed. One of the most important implications of psychoanalysis is that it underscores the force of the social and cultural reproduction of subjects in terms of sexuality and gender. Concomitantly, it points to the anxiety that surrounds transgression at any point along the narrative of 'development'. The axes of identification and desire provide a point of intersection in the narrative of subjects, suggesting a crisis of staging that is never successfully passed through or left behind, but one that retains a level of tension in terms of pleasure and involvement. Contemporary culture bears testimony to this in many ways, from fan cultures (most overtly) in music and football, to broader instances of cultural engagement in shopping, films and television and so on. It is within this framework that I think *Rebecca* poses many questions about the attraction of this blurring of boundaries, and the necessary force of repression; to close the narrative it is necessary to burn the house down, but still the subject is haunted.

The 'boy in the box': outing Du Maurier

The publication in 1993 of Margaret Forster's biography of Du Maurier merited media attention for its disclosure of the author's relationships with women. I am not suggesting however that it is possible to link the reading of *Rebecca* here with the autobiography in a functional way, that Du Maurier's lesbian relationships invite a lesbian reading of her texts. This would problematically pose a sort of authenticity for both the author and the reader. The text of *Rebecca* has been and will continue to be 'written' by readers in varied contexts and in the light of varied knowledges and investments. Rather, Forster's biography of Du Maurier exists here as an intertextual influence, and an opportunity to pose some interesting questions about class and sexuality.

The naturalizing structure of the genre of biography (a linear development of character that becomes increasingly comprehensible) frames Forster's text. Indeed, the book's cover frames the text with this notion of authenticity, claiming that Forster 'strips away' the facade and lays bear the 'true workings' of Du Maurier. Only despite the genre then, does Forster's biography exacerbate some interesting points about Du Maurier's life. The first of these is Du Maurier's own concept of her sexuality. Early in Forster's text we learn that Du Maurier struggles with the diverse focus of her own desire, interestingly seen in terms of gender roles. To desire women from the position of a woman, termed 'Venetian' by Du Maurier, is problematic, while to desire to be a boy (and therefore to desire women) is a notion that can be and is articulated. What is suggested by Du Maurier's own formulation is a type of gender performance, which keeps in play gender opposition across the materiality of bodily 'sexual' difference.

Yet what remains the most poignant feature of the text is the notion of economic security as a necessity for any form of sexual freedom. Like the character Rebecca, Du Maurier manages her own independence from the duties and confined spaces of marriage. The outing of Du Maurier is, on the other hand, wholly unremarkable in the way that it delivers one more aristocratic figure to the history of lesbianism alongside Vita Sackville-West, Virginia Woolf, Radcliff Hall and others. Yet this return of lesbianism to an aristocratic place overlooks the instances of queerness that, I have argued here, exist in many popular cultural forms. The discourses of fandom and the many practices, leisure pursuits and levels of engagement that tread the blurred borderline between desire for and identification with, are described as 'adolescent' but for many people continue into adulthood, albeit in a disguised form. These discourses testify to the widespread fluidity of desire across the spectrum of class, and in an increasingly consumer-orientated context the imbrication of desire and identification is likely to become more complex. 'We' are all invited to buy into this game, be it in different ways and with different levels of sophistication nuanced by factors of class and ethnicity. Sexual ambivalence and same-sex desire are not limited to the aristocratic hall of fame, but are kicking around in the rooms of a different, more commonplace 'home'.

Note

Janet Harbord lectures in cultural studies at Middlesex University.

References

ANG, Ien (1985) *Watching Dallas: Soap Opera and the Melodramatic Imagination* London: Methuen.

—— (1991) *Desperately Seeking the Audience* London: Routledge.
BUTLER, Judith (1990) *Gender Trouble: Feminism and the Subversion of Identity* New York and London: Routledge.
—— (1993) *Bodies That Matter: On the Discursive Limits of Sex* New York and London: Routledge.
DE LAURETIS, Teresa (1991) editor, 'Queer theory: lesbian and gay sexualities' *Differences* Vol. 3, Summer.
DOANE, Mary Ann (1991) *Femmes Fatales: Feminism, Film Theory, Psychoanalysis* New York and London: Routledge.
DOLLIMORE, Jonathan (1991) *Sexual Dissidence: Augustine to Wilde, Freud to Foucault* Clarendon Press: Oxford University Press.
DONALD, James (1991) editor, *Thresholds: Psychoanalysis and Cultural Theory* London: Macmillan.
DU MAURIER, Daphne (1938) *Rebecca* London and Sydney: Pan Books.
FLETCHER, John (1989) 'Freud and his uses: psychoanalysis and gay theory' in **Shepherd** and **Wallis**, editors.
FORSTER, Margaret (1993) *Daphne Du Maurier* London: Arrow.
FREUD, Sigmund (1953) *On Sexuality*, translated James Strachey, Vol. 7, London: The Penguin Freud Library.
GERAGHTY, Christine (1991) *Women and Soap Opera* Cambridge: Polity Press.
GLEDHILL, Christine (1987) *Home Is Where The Heart Is: Studies in Melodrama and the Woman's Film* London: BFI.
JAGOSE, Annamaria (1994) *Lesbian Utopics* London: Routledge.
LIGHT, Alison (1984) '"Returning to Manderley" romance fiction, female sexuality and class' *Feminist Review* No. 16, Summer.
MULVEY, Laura (1975) 'Visual pleasure and narrative cinema' *Screen* Vol. 16, Autumn.
RADWAY, Janice (1984) *Reading the Romance: Women, Patriarchy and Popular Literature* Chapel Hill, NC: University of North Carolina Press.
SEDGWICK, Eve Kosofsky (1985) *Between Men: English Literature and Male Homosocial Desire* New York: Columbia University Press.
—— (1990) *Epistemology of the Closet* Berkeley, CA: University of California Press.
—— (1994) *Tendencies* New York and London: Routledge.
SEITER, Ellen, BORCHERS, Hans, KREUTZNER, Gabriele and WARTH, Eva-Maria (1989) *Remote Control: Television, Audiences and Cultural Power* London and New York: Routledge.
SHEPHERD, Simon and WALLIS, Nick (1989) editors, *Coming on Strong: Gay Politics and Culture* London: Unwin Hyman.
SILVERMAN, Kaja (1991) *Male Subjectivity in the Margins* New York: Routledge.
STACEY, Jackie (1987) 'Desperately seeking difference' *Screen* Vol. 28, Winter.
—— (1993) *Star Gazing: Hollywood Cinema and Female Spectatorship* London: Routledge.

Poem

Claire Nicol

Daisy, Rose and Lily

Pick a flower, girls:

Daisy lies upon the ground
Yellow at the core
Her silky legs she spreads around
Just like a little whore

Nose in air stands Rosy-Red
Pricking all who touch
Her one foot in that dirty bed
Frustrates them very much

Aah . . . Lily-White, who sleeps alone
Her flower fades unseen
At least though, when she's dead and gone
They all know where she's been

Reviews

Becoming a Woman and other Essays in 19th and 20th Century Feminist History
Sally Alexander
Virago Press: London, 1994
ISBN 1 85381 757 0, £16.99 Pbk

The essays which make up *Becoming a Woman* were written over a twenty-year period, between 1974 and 1993. Arranged more or less chronologically, there is a narrative embedded in them: a story of the study of women in our times. The first essay, 'Women's work in nineteenth-century London: a study of the years 1820–60s' is resolutely material, its object being to make working women visible in a history that had hidden them. 'Most historians define the working class *de facto* as working men. . . . The labour historian has ignored women as workers – on the labour market and within the household.' What now seems merely commonsensical in such an opening was then both radical and unsettling. Marxism, gender-blind, nevertheless offered a coherent theoretical baseline of a broadly emancipatory kind for women historians who wanted more than a piecemeal women's history. In the 1950s and 1960s, British Marxist historians of the New Left were reappraising all history, conceptualizing it in a way which could bring in new subjects not previously seen as historical agents. They were enormously influential as writers and teachers. It is not at all surprising that feminist history should have hitched itself to the wagon; nor that the fragmentation of the previously stable category 'Woman' should have contributed to the breakup of what Heidi Hartmann called 'The unhappy marriage of Marxism and Feminism'. The narrative we are offered here enacts that break, and a key essay, 'Women, class and sexual difference in the 1830s and 1840s: some reflections on the writing of a feminist history' engages directly with it. The overall trajectory of the collection takes us from the material to the subjective; from exteriority to interiority; from the concrete to the fantastic; from the economic to the unconscious; from what is to what is felt to be; from how things are to the meaning of what they seem; from a Marxist history to psychoanalysis.

Questions to do with relationships of production and property give way to 'a concept of the subject divided by sex and driven by phantasy and the unconscious as well as economic need'. In pursuit of this subject who is no subject (for 'history has no Subject'), language takes on a pre-eminence at the centre of enquiry that class once had. Some of the writing in the later essays reads like speech, which is perhaps not accidental. It reflects a preoccupation with women's speech as revelatory of the unconscious, itself offering clues to the experiential, of what it means to be female, how femaleness is lived differently (in the body as well as in speech) at different historical times. The psychic may be more resistant to change than our social selves, but it is an article of faith here that it should be as open to historical investigation as were the weekly wages of hatters or needlewomen.

This is a rich and many layered collection of writings, indispensable for anyone who wants to understand how feminist history has developed over the last twenty years. It contains essays which have been inspirational to many over the years and which will now rightly find a new and enthusiastic readership. There is an openness of tone and commitment to clarity about debates and issues which is very welcome. Feminist historians have tended to embrace the autobiographical, and Sally Alexander is no exception, using the personal as a touchstone. But for the most part she is clearly more comfortable making her points about women's lives through the lives of others. These are the essays which least stand the test of time. The interviews with Yvonne Kapp, 'Becoming a woman in London in the 1920s and 1930s' and 'Memory, generation and history', are attempts to rethink periodicity by working through women's memories of how they lived and how they yearned to live. The unhappy marriage here is a stylistic one, between the demotic and the academic. Oral testimonies which express their meaning perfectly well are gathered into generalizations, taken by the researcher/historian and served up for another audience altogether. Striving for documentary truthfulness produces, paradoxically, an unintended condescension. As others have discovered, reaching for the truth of personal selves demands a different kind of writing, not necessarily the endlessly destabilized language of Lacanian theory, but a language Sally Alexander gestures towards when she speaks of imaginary power and the idioms of poetry or colloquial speech.

In the early days, Marxist historians argued that the unconscious was universal, ahistorical and unchanging, and thus not relevant to historical enquiry. Feminists argued that sexual difference is rooted in the unconscious, and that the arrangements of sexual/social ordering are prompted by unconscious drives and desires. Appropriately, then, the 'I' here, having travelled that journey, is a confessedly uncertain one by the second half of the volume: unsure, as many of us are, where the emphasis on subjectivities will take a feminism no longer attached to political activism, and busily proliferating into hybrid forms in the wider world as well as in the academy.

Norma Clarke

Antisemitism, Misogyny and the Logic of Cultural Difference: Cesare Lombroso and Matilde Serao

Nancy A. Harrowitz
University of Nebraska Press: Lincoln and London, 1994
ISBN 8032 2374 9, £13.99

This book is less about 'the logic of cultural difference' replayed through misogyny and antisemitism than a close historical account of its exhibition through the work of two key writers. The setting is late nineteenth-century Italy, and the analysis primarily concerns Cesare Lombroso, founding father of modern criminology, and Matilde Serao, prolific novelist, journalist and (apparent, though Harrowitz suggests not uniformly) vociferous anti-feminist. The analytical starting point is that antisemitism and misogyny are bound together in these nineteenth-century discourses through the effort to contain and control difference, and Lombroso and Serao both not only theorize these differences but also exemplify prevalent strategies for dealing with them.

As well as considering the influence of their ideas, at issue is how these authors collude with antisemitism and misogyny to address their own social marginalization. That is, not only how they indulge in a 'betrayal of self-identity' (p. 13) by derogating their own group (Lombroso as a Jew, Serao as a woman), but conversely, how vilification of the other (misogyny for Lombroso, antisemitism for Serao) works to secure their participation within the dominant group. In the penultimate chapter, through a close reading of Serao's novels, it is suggested that this is no mere substitution of category of oppression, but rather that representations of gender, culture and religion have to be understood as mutually elaborated. Thus Serao's texts offer a critique of patriarchy only by portraying its evils as associated with the male Jew, while the difference of Jewish women is safely secured by the (characteristic) plot device of having them convert to Christianity and therefore qualify as sexually available.

Such specificity lends the analysis a strength sometimes lacking in accounts of the relations between racism and sexism. Moreover, the particular attention to the reciprocal dynamics of antisemitism and misogyny through the writings of these authors clarifies the role of historical and cultural context in their forms. However, the danger of this focus on the particular is that the dynamics of anxiety, fear and derision can become too closely interpreted in terms of the personal histories of the figures concerned. Tendencies towards such reductionism from text to author are at moments discernible in the middle chapters of the book (as in the speculations about Lombroso's fixation on circumcision, or the claim that he 'makes the connection between Jews and prostitutes just as often as he can' (p. 57)). More generally, though, this is warded off by the framing of the book within an account of the emergence of modern scientific discourse as central to biologically based accounts of racial and female inferiority. The fable of 'the taint of the quagga', with which the book opens, nicely portrays the interconnections between these accounts. This mythical theory, which Darwin briefly subscribed to but which was developed further by his younger cousin and architect of eugenics, Francis Galton, claimed that the progeny of a female is inevitably influenced by her first breeding. This thus combined anxieties around paternity and the sexual control of women with the racialist discourse of miscegenation. That both, as Harrowitz suggests, arise from a similar source at the founding moment of modern western science is worth remembering in the light of subsequent rhetorics of science in the service of racism (including antisemitism) and misogyny.

A valuable feature of the book is its explicit refusal of the deterministic and monolithic designations of 'self-hatred' which, as the author points out, have been particularly applied to Jews. These not only invite individualized accounts in terms of personal pathology that abstract antisemitism and misogyny from cultural-political conditions, but thereby also lapse into victim-blaming. Rather, Harrowitz prefers the term 'self-abnegation' to cover a variety of stances of devaluation or distancing, and distinguishes between 'Jewish antisemitism' and 'Jewish self-hatred'. She explores some well-known candidates, including Karl Marx and cultural anthropologist Franz Boas before considering Otto Weininger (Jewish convert to Protestantism, and author of the antisemitic and misogynist *Sex and Character*), and usefully situates these within an account of the circulation of ideas to show how 'Lombroso's ideas about difference in women, criminals and Jews contributed to an atmosphere in Italy that at the turn of the century was receptive to Weininger and hostile to Freud' (p. 74).

While generally well-structured and clearly argued, there is an asymmetry in the treatment of Lombroso in relation to the influence of his ideas on women and Jews respectively. Further, the analysis of his complicity with antisemitism lacks a class analysis which intersects also with existing cultural tensions between Sephardic and Ashkenazi Jews. In terms of the role of science in naturalizing both antisemitism and misogyny, the narrative at times lapses into charges of false claims to science rather than consistently portraying science as central to the regulation and production of difference, as in, for example, Lombroso 'derails outright the scientific methodology employed in his work' (p. 58). Ultimately, while fascinating in its juxtapositions and specificities, these are at the expense of consideration of broader questions. The reader is left no clearer about what commonalities and relations there might be between antisemitism and misogyny in the premodern period, or outside Europe. But what we do gain is a closer understanding of their particular intertwinings and conditions inside, and a thoughtful exploration of the production of racialized and gendered identities.

Erica Burman

New Right Discourse on Race and Sexuality: Britain 1968–1990
Anna Marie Smith
Cambridge University Press: Cambridge, 1994
ISBN 0 521 45921 4, £12.95/$17.95 Pbk
ISBN 1 521 45297 X, £37.50/$59.95 Hbk

This book's cover proclaims *New Right Discourse on Race and Sexuality* as 'a groundbreaking study of racism and homophobia in British politics, which demonstrates the demonization of blacks, lesbians and gays in New Right Discourse'. Focusing primarily on the emergence and 'hegemonization' of Thatcherism throughout the 1980s, Anna Marie Smith seeks to demonstrate the centrality of issues of 'race' and (homo)sexuality to the success of the Thatcherite project through theoretical analysis of what she argues are two key moments: the immigration debates of the late 1960s, notably the infamous speeches of Enoch Powell, and the debates about the promotion of homosexuality articulated around the Section 28 legislation of 1987–88.

With an uneasy combination of literary and cultural theory and historical case study, Smith has three objectives: first, to put racism and homophobia on the agenda of political science as 'symbolic nodal points rather than isolated "issues"' (p. 17); second, to demonstrate the complexity of these discourses; and third, to explore the 'genealogical' (p. 22) relations between the two discourses – which means simply, for Smith, how the demonization of the gay community was founded on the previous demonizations of black immigrants. Focusing on 'the nation' and 'the family' – which are seen as distinct arenas – Smith uses theories from Lacan, Derrida, Nietzsche and Foucault to assert the by now familiar trope of the 'outsider' through and against which boundaries are imagined, enacted and legislated.

It is perhaps fair to argue that it is the exploration of theories of discourse, rather than 'race' or sexuality, that forms the substance of Smith's book. It could be argued further that the wealth of theory ultimately masks rather than reveals the complexities of either of these discourses, reiterating ideological ground already won rather than extending it. A welter of jargon serves to obscure an argument that is high on assertion and repetition and frustratingly scarce on detail. Although Smith makes some interesting comparisons with the United States, on the whole her argument employs stridency at the expense of substance, reducing the complexity of New Right discourse to a series of undemonstrated statements, political exhortations and ahistorical over-simplifications. In the process, and most notably in regard to 'race', she reinscribes the marginality of the categories she claims to be deconstructing.

Thus, Smith's analysis of the demonization of black communities focuses exclusively on immigration, reducing and denying the complex of images of exclusion that operate internally to the imagined nation – in employment, law and order, the family and education. Her appropriation of Stuart Hall's and Paul Gilroy's work here has lost or simply abandoned the nuanced and polysemous manifestations of the trope of 'the immigrant' in British racial discourse in favour of a uni-dimensional figure placed firmly at the boundary of the nation. This then allows Smith to argue for an understanding of discourses around homosexuality as a complementary element – a construction of homosexuals as 'the enemy within', a threat to the otherwise homogeneous British 'family' in the same way as black people are a threat to its outer limits. The careless exclusion of black people from this British family in Smith's own analysis is made clear in her concluding assertion that:

> For every brutal deployment of colonizing strategies, there was persecution of an Oscar Wilde or some other sexual/gender deviant in the 'mother country';

for every Falklands or Gulf War, there will be many more rapes and queer-bashings 'back home' (p. 242).

What seems not to have occurred to Smith is that a Gulf War abroad could translate to *racial* attacks at home, because within her schema, black people in Britain are never 'at home'. Moreover, to assert simply that the representation of homosexuality reflects and extends that of black people lacks both explanatory power (after all, 'othering' is a standard feature of discourses around class, ethnic and religious minorities, women and so on) and a clearly articulated historical dimension. If 1980s constructions of homosexuality employed motifs familiar from 1950s racial discourse, it is also true that Powellism was founded upon a history of racial theory and colonialism dating back at least to the Enlightenment, and that contemporary constructions of homosexuality owe a debt to nineteenth-century reifications of sexuality.

More importantly, Smith's account of contemporary discourse has failed to fully recognize the ways in which discourses of 'race' and sexuality, nation and family are intimately connected. Theories of hypersexuality, fertility and desire are at the heart of racial discourse, and vice versa (for example, 'race' becomes a primary signifier of the AIDS crisis), while it seems inconceivable to think of conservative approaches to 'the family' without taking account of the racialization of single and teenage parenthood and the familial schisms caused by racist immigration legislation. The family and sexuality are figured as white throughout; black homosexuality remains, as so often, invisible.

The reductionism of Smith's approach throughout the book ultimately constructs the authoritarianism she herself admits (p. 243) as unidimensional and unproblematic in its inception and enactment. This not only denies the multifarious and adaptive forms of New Right discourse which yield much of its 'hegemonic' strength, but silences the forms of resistance which remain so crucial to the groups thus situated and circumscribed. In her celebration of discourse, Smith has lost sight of its subjects.

Claire Alexander

Alcohol, Gender and Culture

Edited by Dimitra Gefou-Madianou

Routledge: London, 1992
ISBN 0 415 08667 1, £35.00 Hbk

'Europeans, who constitute $12\frac{1}{2}$ per cent of the world's population, consume 50 per cent of the recorded world production of alcohol.' With this striking statistic, Dimitra Gefou-Madianou opens a discussion, focusing on European societies, on the sociological dimensions of alcohol consumption: its social and ceremonial uses, its role in cultural, religious and social identities, and in particular, the ways it is manipulated, practically and symbolically, to constitute, signify and challenge gender relations. Nine anthropologists present material from Greece, Spain, France, Hungary, Sweden, Ireland and Egypt, obtained during extended fieldwork in particular communities. Unlike previous studies, the authors do not, a priori, posit drinking as a social problem in need of eradication or management; rather, their more open-ended investigations demonstrate that the way alcohol affects the mind and body is as much a social and cultural as a physiological matter.

The emphasis on alcohol as a component of commensality, used to establish solidarity, create and mediate boundaries and mark or mask social distinctions, is not surprising, and the influences of Emile Durkheim and Mary Douglas are ubiquitous in these papers. In the majority of the societies described, distinctions of gender, age, class, region, occupation and even political orientation are asserted by one's choice of drink and manner of imbibing, although the meaning of the drink may further vary according to the time of day, the setting and the company in which it is consumed. Virtually all the authors show a mastery of this arena of local knowledge. They bring, however, particular anthropological concerns to bear upon this material and thus move beyond mere description. Michael Stewart's exhilarating analysis of Hungarian Vlach Gypsy drinking practices, and the different meanings and uses of brandy, beer and water – among men and women, family and outsiders, Gypsy and non-Gypsy – is deepened by his attention to Gypsy notions of the body and bodily substances, since the body marks social boundaries and registers transgressions of these. In a careful, if at points speculative, argument he suggests that Gypsy social identity, formally expressed among groups of men and conceptualized in a male idiom of 'brotherhood', is constructed in commensal situations through eschewing food (associated with individual households) and instead sharing drink and song. Dimitra Gefou-Madianou's analysis of the gender dynamics and symbolism in the production and consumption of wine and spirits in a Greek agrotown posits a certain gender complementarity within an overall context of male domination. Thus women, excluded as 'polluting' from the production of retsina, none the less retain power through their control over the production and distribution of sweet wine, seen as essential to male fertility. Prodigious and lovingly rendered ethnographic detail enables her to document the multiple, complex and shifting expressions of unity and exclusion – between and among women and men, families, growers and Athenian merchants – manifested in making and drinking alcohol.

The gender and religious symbolism of wine production and consumption is further developed in two additional papers. Working in the Alsace region, Isabelle Bianquis-Gasser describes wine as a 'sacred' substance associated with both fertility and death. She documents the gender division of labour involved in planting and tending vines, harvesting grapes, producing wine and drinking it, and its determination by the symbolism of the Christian calendar through which the vine cycle is conceptualized. A. Marina Iossifides' gracefully written account focuses on the meanings of wine in the context of Holy Communion for a community of Orthodox nuns in northwest Greece, and its role in representing relations between the secular and religious, body and soul, female and male. It draws on ethnographic data from both convent and neighbouring village to argue that the Eucharistic symbolism, whereby the sharing of wine constitutes a community of believers, pervades the everyday uses of and attitudes towards wine and even other alcoholic drinks. In the societies examined in these four papers, where – as the editor phrases it – 'alcohol is interwoven into the matrix of [people's] personal, social and religious lives', inebriation may be a highly valued state, social as much as chemical in its genesis (thus do Hungarian gypsies get drunk on weak beer, and Greeks, when necessary, on water). In the face of such complex operations between the body and society, generic epidemiological definitions of alcoholism seem crude and unhelpful.

The extent to which drinking remains a predominantly single-sex activity is striking, though authors acknowledge that this is starting to change. Three papers which focus on male drinking reveal that similarities in practice do not guarantee similarities in meaning. Henk Driessen's brief but wide-ranging paper on alcohol and gender in Andalusia, which touches on drinking etiquette, religion, and changing and contradictory gender ideas and practices, ponders why men drink both competitively and more than women, and suggests that men drink, among other reasons, to obfuscate their dependence on women and their weak economic and social position in local society. By contrast, placing the economic implications of drinking at the centre of his analysis, Adrian Peace argues that among the fishermen of 'Clontarf', Ireland, involvement in the social world of the bar is in itself crucial for economic survival and success. Here fishermen gather information, rehearse fishing strategies, assert personal and professional prowess, experience sociability and construct identities. Peace's rendition of the interlacing of drinking, fishing, masculinity and 'Pier' identity, and how these shape social experience and the understandings of self and society, evinces both deep familiarity with his material and exceptional subtlety of analysis. Gunilla Bjerén's portrait of drinking and masculinity in everyday life in a Swedish logging and administrative town is of particular interest as an example of a society with deeply ambivalent attitudes to alcohol, and one where the state intervenes actively in an attempt to control its consumption. Drunkenness among men is shaped by tensions between Swedish values of authenticity and self-disclosure, on the one hand, and sobriety and self-control on the other. Women who drink, however, 'are playing with dynamite' since drunkenness in a woman is not easily forgiven.

Two fascinating but very different papers follow up this theme of female drinking and transgression. Karin van Nieuwkerk looks at the strategies of female entertainers in Egypt to defend their moral reputations, control their working conditions and even economically prosper while working in, by definition, 'disreputable' establishments. Islamic suspicion of altered states of consciousness underpins the condemnation of alcohol and tobacco for both sexes, but a woman's supposedly weaker control over her sensuality makes her the more heartily condemned. Although many female entertainers survive by very publicly refraining from these intoxicants, a few defiantly indulge in them precisely in order to be counted as honorary 'men' who other men dare not tamper with. Eleni Papagaroufali, inspired by Foucault's notion of 'games of power and pleasure', examines the drinking practices of urban Greek feminists in the early 1980s, both in the traditionally male spaces of bars and tavernas, and in the female-defined space of the Women's Coffeehouse in Athens. She is concerned to draw out the transformational potentialities of women's transgressive acts, brilliantly elucidating how female appropriations of male prerogatives are not simply claims to equal and identical pleasures but produce their own specific pleasures of confrontation, self-definition and alternative world-making. Her paper distinguishes itself from others of this panegyric but sometimes empirically ungrounded 'female transgression and resistence' genre of analysis by her attention to the specificities and contradictions of the two dominant feminist ideologies embraced by her feminist subjects and, here, enacted and explored through alcohol use.

Although varying in ethnographic depth and analytic panache, the papers should interest feminist readers in their documentation both of the cultural logics and social practices which link gender and alcohol in particular ways in diverse European contexts, and of women's not infrequent gestures to oppose, resist or wrest control of the dominant cultural and social order through drinking, be they feminists, monastics or even 'proper women'.

Jane K. Cowan

Gender Politics and Post-Communism: Reflections from Eastern Europe and the Former Soviet Union
Edited by Nanette Funk and Magda Mueller
Routledge: London, 1993
ISBN 0 415 90478 1 Pbk, ISBN 0 415 90477 3 Hbk

Cinderella Goes to Market: Citizenship, Gender and Women's Movements in East Central Europe
Barbara Einhorn
Verso: London, 1993
ISBN 0 86091 615 4 Pbk, ISBN 0 86091 410 0 Hbk

As those working in the field will know, over the last year or two there has been a steady stream of volumes devoted to the subject of women/gender during the post-communist period in Eastern Europe and the former Soviet Union. The two books under review are at the forefront of these. Barbara Einhorn's book is unusual as it represents the work of a single author who has a relatively long-standing interest in gender issues in Eastern Europe. Funk and Mueller's book, in contrast, is an edited volume which brings together contributions from as many as thirty-five authors from both East and West. In fact, the voices of women activists, researchers and writers from throughout Eastern Europe and the former Soviet Union fill the pages of both books. This is welcome and brings a repetition of themes which in itself is significant, given the diversity of the pre-communist pasts and post-communist futures of the countries involved. Inevitably, it is the worsening experience of many women in this part of the world which is the object of concern, with a number of persistent questions underlying the accounts presented. What was it about state socialism that gave rise to such consistent patterns of gender relations in the Soviet Bloc? How is one to understand the widespread deterioration of the position of many women in all post-communist countries and what is 'the legacy of communism' in this regard? In what way do women themselves contribute to or challenge these trends? Why is there such a strikingly consistent rejection in all post-communist societies of what we might want to term 'feminism'? Indeed, as Einhorn (p. 14) asks, 'Does the widespread current East Central European "allergy" to feminism imply the need for a revision or at least a rethink of Western feminist concepts?'

The two books provide a wealth of information and commentary and will be, if they are not already, part of the required reading in the field. In Einhorn's book, the reader will find excellent accounts of what is happening to Eastern European women with respect to politics and employment (in her chapter entitled 'Where have all the women gone?'), as well as a useful account of reproductive rights ('Self-determination under threat'). There is also a chapter on feminism in Eastern Europe, where the gulf between East and West is epitomized by the experience of women in the two Germanies:

> A deep chasm formed by very different life experience, different discourse, different concepts and consciousness separated them, a divide which has been termed 'the Wall in our heads'. This discovery stunned women in the two parts of Germany and began what has proved to be a long and tortuous process of mutual acquaintance beset by severe problems of communication.
> (Einhorn, p. 204)

The contributions to the Funk and Mueller volume are organized by country, with a final section on 'Reflections from the outside'. There is some unavoidable overlap here with the material covered by Einhorn, but the contributions are wide-ranging and engaging. The plurality of viewpoints put forward in both books makes a unified assessment difficult in the space of a short review. In general, though, it has to be said that the questions which underlie the texts remain largely open. That is because this new field is as yet rather poorly theorized. It is not the aim of either book to provide such a theory; indeed, Einhorn is quite clear about this from the outset: her study, she says, 'does not aim to prescribe solutions to the big questions' (p. 15).

One part of an explanation of gender relations in post-communist society must be a coming to terms with the 'legacy of communism', what Einhorn calls the 'ambiguity' of women's position under state socialism, the 'double burden' of paid work and domestic labour that prompts the 'Cinderella' in the title of her book. Yet as Olga Tóth in the Funk and Mueller volume urges, we also need to get beyond the 'pity' we feel for the Eastern European woman so characterized. If we are to do this, we will have to expand accounts of social policy and the sexual division of labour to include considerations of cultural context (a number of authors intimate as much). For the often implicit assumption in such accounts is that the ambiguity of women's position under communism could have been resolved by a more thorough-going public policy of female emancipation. Would extending communist legislation 'beyond the garden gate' really have brought 'liberation' and gender equality? Enikö Bollobás, in her chapter entitled 'Totalitarian lib: the legacy of communism for Hungarian women', seems to think it would. She also appears to argue that virtually all women's misfortunes in post-communism can be explained in terms of the shortcomings of the communist 'emancipation' of women. But Hana Havelková is right when she says that 'Explaining patriarchy directly by appeal to the paternalism of the totalitarian regime is an all too easy and short-circuited approach' (Havelková/Funk and Mueller, p. 69). In her extremely interesting contribution to the same volume, Joanna Goven illustrates the truth of Havelková's remark by diagnosing and documenting the antifeminism of antipolitics in Hungary. The 'legacy of communism' is clearly an extremely complex issue and still in many ways an unknown quantity. But whatever this legacy turns out to be, it is clear that it can only be one part of an explanation of the current reordering of gender relations and has to be considered in tandem with a real/imagined liberal democracy which is the other side of what is happening now in post-communist societies. A critical attitude to really existing democracy is also needed if it is to be 'reinvented', as Zilla Eisenstein (Funk and Mueller, p. 307) calls for. This criticism is still at times worryingly lacking. Consider the following excerpt, whose author was for many years Professor of American Studies in Budapest:

> The various benefits women enjoyed in the communist societies, such as full employment, free health care, maternity leave, and cheap abortion, only sound appealing to foreign observers, to whom the words have different and much more positive meanings. In Hungarian – as well as Czech Slovak, Polish, and Russian – these words sound pitiful, cheap, poor, gloomy, because that is the reality they evoke. When in Hungary we hear about full employment, we know that it has the effect of killing ambition and initiative in millions of people, and that it masked unemployment. When we hear about free health care we do not picture an American hospital but an overcrowded, undermanned, underequipped, underdeveloped Eastern European hospital. When we hear about maternity leave we know how much it pays and that the practice generates underachievement.

(Bollobás/Funk and Mueller, p. 203)

The point here is not that the gloominess did not exist, nor that in retrospect some of it might be fading, but rather that unemployment and lack of maternity benefits, indeed the disastrous American health care system, are deproblematized at a stroke. The passage may also give some hint of a reason for the resistance to feminism which has been so widely noted in post-communist society – for, in pointing to the thwarted ambition and initiative of millions of 'people', is the author not also very close to expressing a gendered concern for the 'ghostly and fictitious' men of state socialism which Larissa Lissyutkina, for example, describes in her chapter entitled 'Soviet women at the crossroads of perestroika' (Lissyutkina/Funk and Mueller, p. 283)?

Peggy Watson

Straight Sex: The Politics of Pleasure
Lynne Segal
Virago: London, 1994
ISBN 1 85381 802 X, £8.99

Lynne Segal's aim in this book is to challenge what she sees as current feminist orthodoxy: namely the idea that heterosexuality is the basis of men's exploitation of women, and the related notion that lesbianism is the most authentic expression of feminist politics. According to Segal, feminists have had almost nothing to say about love or desire, and, by their silence, have allowed a few very visible feminists to set the agenda. Segal paints a bleak picture of both the apparent lack of debate among feminists, and the ability of contemporary feminism to speak to the experiences of the vast majority of heterosexual women. She depicts a repressive atmosphere, the tone of which was set by campaigns against pornography, in which women feel unable to talk about sexual pleasure.

The purpose of *Straight Sex* is to challenge this. Segal argues that alongside confident lesbian and gay campaigns around sexuality, we need reversals of the dominant, phallic constructions of heterosexuality: 'Instead of guilt-tripping heterosexual women, feminists would do better to enlist them in the "queering" of traditional understanding of gender and sexuality' (p. xv). Straight sex, Segal asserts, may be no more affirmative of normative gender positions than gay and lesbian sex.

The book begins with Segal's own sexual and political formation in the 1960s. The story told is a familiar one; the trajectory traced is one from a time when women saw sex as liberation to one in which they sought liberated sex. The second chapter takes up the story at this point, outlining the disagreements between feminists about the nature of men's domination. Here Segal draws on themes developed in her other books, to argue that the preoccupation with sexual violence, rape and pornography lead to a kind of essentialism and ahistoricism in much feminist thought, and a sense of the *inevitability* of men's exploitation of women. In her words, 'the tendency simply to blame men . . . was soon to overtake the passion to reform them' (p. 49). Chapters 3 and 4 review the literatures of sex research and psychoanalysis respectively, and Chapter 5 examines the contribution made to feminism by queer theory and practice. The final chapters are devoted to Segal's attempt to rethink heterosexuality in such a way as to challenge dominant and oppressive constructions of it.

Like all Segal's books, *Straight Sex* is beautifully written. She is a meticulous researcher, but handles complex ideas so fluently that she is able to render them easily accessible without losing any of their subtlety or nuances. Her discussions of psychoanalytic theory and of Judith Butler's work will become fixtures on my undergraduate reading lists for this reason. The book is a pleasure to read and is considerably enriched by the fragments of feminist poetry which illustrate many of her discussions. Overall, then, *Straight Sex* deserves much more attention than I am able to give it in this short review. In the remainder I will focus on a few aspects of the book which I found disquieting.

The first thing which troubled me was the way Segal set up the argument, as a challenge to feminist orthodoxy. Perhaps I am too young, do not mix in the 'right' circles, or am not sufficiently well-read, but I simply did not recognize her portrait of feminism's dominant line on heterosexuality. The attribution of orthodoxy seemed to rest primarily upon a couple of rather old titles, which in no way reflect the dynamism and diversity of opinion of the feminism that I know. The repressive atmosphere of being guilt-tripped and silenced by other feminists about being straight is not one which I regularly encounter. So, on the one hand, this portrayal simply did not 'ring true' for me. But perhaps more significantly, I am troubled by the very use of the idea of a feminist orthodoxy. It seems to me that to claim this is not simply to misrepresent feminism, but to play into the hands of our critics – by reinforcing their conviction that feminism is a rigid, dogmatic line to which strict adherence is required, and which silences or marginalizes dissenters from the orthodoxy.

My unease about Segal's assertion of feminist orthodoxy does not make me reject her argument. Nevertheless, there are aspects of it which I find extremely problematic. One criticism is of Segal's understanding of discourse. The book is influenced by a Foucauldian reading of sexuality, and a questioning of – if not scepticism about – the idea of a pre-discursive body. Yet Segal is inconsistent about the status she accords to discourse, and seems unable to decide whether it is a true account or whether a layer of ideology (for example, cultural constructions of romance) has somehow intervened. More importantly, the relationship of ordinary people's discourse to broader historical constructions is not made clear.

Never is this more problematic than when the discourse at issue is women's accounts of whether they do or do not like heterosexual intercourse. Segal is scathing about Shere Hite's work, gleefully reproducing the positive statements which many of Hite's interviewees made about sex with men, in order to demonstrate Hite's bias in her reading of the result. But what Segal does not seem to recognize is that there can be many – not just one – discourses about sex, and that these are differently rewarded and sanctioned in our culture. It may be that Hite's respondents, in saying (as many of them did) that they didn't orgasm during penetrative sex but they loved it anyway, were reproducing a very traditional and socially valued discourse. It is not that this is in any sense a 'lie', or an example of 'false consciousness', but rather that sex – like most things – is constructed and lived through a *multiplicity of discourses*, not just one.

It seems to me that Segal is more ambivalent than she acknowledges about how much women enjoy heterosexual sex. The picture she presents is largely a very optimistic, up-beat one – there are many women getting an awful lot of pleasure from having sex with men, and they should damn well not have to apologize for it, she seems to be saying. Fine. But occasionally cracks appear in this argument, as when she acknowledges 'many women's disappointment with sex' (p. 241), or what a let-down the experience of heterosexual intercourse is for many young women. Segal rightly chastizes some researchers for letting their own assumptions inhibit their ability to recognize the very real pleasures which young women are obtaining from straight sex, but I cannot feel happy about the way she treats women's claims to gain pleasure (sometimes solely) from their partner's pleasure as unproblematic. Voyeuristic desire is fine, but if that's all you have and you want more. . . .

Finally, I want to turn to Segal's main argument, namely her belief in the transgressive potential of heterosexual sex. For Segal, sexual relations between men and women threaten, rather than stabilize, gender polarity. Despite being the central argument of the book, the justifications for this claim are rather vague, but they have to do with the loss of control and the vulnerability which Segal says occur during sex: '[S]ex places "manhood" in jeopardy, with its masculine ideal of autonomous selfhood threatened by the self-abnegation, the self-obliteration, that sexual desire engenders' (p. 254). This is where I part company decisively with Segal. It is not that I think that this never happens, but what I object to is the way Segal suddenly projects one, unitary meaning on to sex – sex is about loss of control, it is about blurring the boundaries of the self – when she has argued throughout that this cannot be sustained. Sex may have this meaning for some people at some time, but Segal cannot pronounce that this is what sexual desire is – as if it had some unproblematic essence. I am also uncomfortable with the terms she uses: these notions of transcendence are far too mystical for my liking, and they seem to idealize sexual relations. Her accounts of desire and of sex seem, by the end of the book, to have taken on an almost free-floating quality – abstracted from the social context of power relations in which they exist.

Rosalind Gill

Rethinking Sexual Harassment

Edited by Clare Brant and Yun Lee Too
Pluto Press: London, 1994
ISBN 0 7453 0838 4, £14.95 Pbk, ISBN 0 7453 0837 6, £45.00 Hbk

This book 'aims to raise consciousness about the discourse of sexual harassment and the adequacy of practice based on this language' (p. 2). It has, in this sense, a simple aim, informed by the view that the way in which discourses of sexual harassment are framed makes an important difference politically. However, that is the only overarching narrative this book provides, because it is about using detail and local analysis: 'the contributors . . . show how simplified narratives and explanations of harassment disguise complexity for particular social reasons' (p. 2). The contributors represent a wide range of disciplinary perspectives, noticeably more humanities- than social science-based (history, art, cultural studies, law, women's studies, classics, anthropology and English), but they are all working in academic institutions except one, Ros Hunt, who is a priest.

These authors largely succeed in revealing complexity through working with situated examples: legal and para-legal discourses, the colonial shaping of 'Eve-teasing' in India, British men and women's systematically different accounts of the same incidents of sexual harassment, institutional contexts such as the Anglican church and British universities, lesbian harassment and the visual and textual narratives of the sexuality of 'Asian babes' for male consumption in the British Midlands. Local discourses are scrutinized, 'deconstructed' and subjected to feminist critiques; critiques which share the merit of not using a 'totalising rhetoric as a polemical strategy' (p. 4) – a phrase used by the editors in describing radical feminist perspectives on sexual harassment. While power is ubiquitous in these accounts, it is not treated as singular or monolithic and can permit the kind of analysis – some would say optimistically – that is suggestive of how feminism can make further gains in the struggle against sexual harassment. For example, Ruth Jamieson discusses how the Canadian Criminal Code stipulates that 'the consent to sexual activity can no longer be assumed, presumed or "believed" unless reasonable steps have been taken to ascertain that consent has in fact been given' (p. 116).

Many chapters reflect the editors' intention of breaking down the category distinctions between sexual harassment and cognate arenas of sexual politics such as date rape, child sexual abuse and pornography as part of an attempt to question and debate the narrow definitions of sexual harassment which have resulted from its development within employment discourses and practices concerning equal opportunities and equal rights. The book's cover photograph likewise represents a broadening of the typical idea of sexual harassment by depicting a woman, not in an office, but walking along a street, briefcase in hand, while a group of men, dressed in working jeans and site helmets, collusively ogle after her. However, Jane Beckett's discussion of this photograph does not reflect what I read as the class dimension of this encounter. On the other hand, Padma Anagol-McGinn introduces a parallel race dimension in her analysis of the colonial context of the history of sexual harassment in India.

In an excellent introductory chapter, Clare Brant and Yun Lee Too map out the field of sexual harassment, historically, politically, and in particular discursively, with a breadth and insight which is clarifying, at the same time as observing their own strictures of multiplicity and rejection of simplification. Their mandatory tour of the contents of the book also follows these principles: rather than treating the contents in linear fashion, author by author, they return to the chapters, surveying them from different angles, weaving strands, shunning the grand narrative.

How well does this 'postmodern' strategy work in 'rethinking sexual harassment'? (While nowhere in this book is an explicit claim to postmodernism made, it seems to me that such principles do inform the editors' approach.) The contributions largely live up to the claims of local analysis, difference and complexity and make accessible reading (often aided by the integration of the writer's reflexivity on the issue). The editors' strategy of organizing the book into three parts – stories, categories and contexts – seems consistent with their wish to challenge more conventional categorizations, although for me it did not contribute anything to the individual chapters.

What about the editors' claim to address practice, as well as discourse? Postmodern feminism has been criticized for potentially undermining the unity of purpose of feminist politics through its emphasis on the local, the diverse, and the multiple and contradictory workings of power. Significantly, therefore, there is no sign of these undermining its political awareness or its political contribution. On the contrary, I found it helpful that the book consistently avoids totalizing accounts of harassment. An edited collection such as this – often regarded with suspicion by publishers because of its potential lack of coherence – works well as a vehicle for such an approach, as long as the diversity of contributions is given sufficient structure by a coherent editorial vision. Understandably, the editorial vision is most apparent in the introductory chapter (written by Brant and Too), but none the less, at its best, this book provides a good model of postmodern political writing within an academic feminist tradition.

Wendy Hollway

Medicine and Nursing. Professions in a Changing Health Service

Sylvia Walby, June Greenwell, Lesley Mackay and Keith Soothill

Sage Publications: London, 1994
ISBN 0 8039 8742 0, £11.95 Pbk, ISBN 0 8039 8741 2 Hbk

This book attempts to bring together important strands in the sociology of work, the sociology of the professions, gender issues, and the sociology of health, in order to examine recent social policy decisions and changes in the British National Health Service. The most important feature of the text is its thorough and consistent review of the literature which brings together all the different strands of thinking. We feel the strength of the book also turns out to be the cause of some of its weaker points. In trying to deal with so much material, the authors at times lose track of their argument. We feel this particularly to be the case when they are relating their empirical work (based on 262 interviews with doctors and nurses working on acute hospital wards) to the main theories which they present. The main themes are the impact of Fordism and post-Fordism on certain groups of workers in the health service, the perceptions of doctors and nurses in relation to the shifting boundaries between their professions, the strategies of professionalization in nursing including primary nursing and Project 2000, and gender issues within the NHS, which is the largest employer in the UK.

The book is well structured with useful signposts and excellent summaries. After a general introduction which sets the scene with an account of Fordism and post-Fordist styles of management, and a discussion of some of the issues of interest concerning inter-professional work in a context of professionalization, there are individual chapters on specific issues. Chapter 2 demonstrates that a division between care and treatment is an inadequate base on which to distinguish between professions, and looks at how the professionalization strategy of nursing is advancing but at the same time is also limited by the profession itself, mainly because of its emphasis on rule-bound behaviour. The third chapter takes a theoretical context, drawing on the sociology of the professions, and explores some of the contradictions that have arisen in the search for efficiencies in an environment of cost containment. Chapter 4 considers the Fordist influences in hospital management, and contrasts the situations within two different hospitals. Chapter 5 looks at issues relating to the management of professional workers, and Chapter 6 considers the extent to which the NHS can be said to be moving towards post-Fordism. The people who will benefit most from this book are students from the various disciplines on which it touches, the sociology of work and of the professions and those in applied health service studies including professional education.

There is much that we found useful in this book. Our main disappointment is that although the authors claim to give much emphasis to gender issues, and allude to gender from time to time throughout the book, we do not feel they adequately address important structural as well as psycho-social issues. They do not, in our view, adequately develop their analysis of the social construction of occupations along gender lines, nor of the hierarchical nature of both professions and the closure within professions of posts which carry real power. It is a striking feature of their empirical data that nursing is trying to get more status and power for itself by assuming a 'male' view of work. It is reclaiming power by taking on technical tasks instead of trying to get higher status in society for caring work. It also seems inevitable that the 'lower status' tasks including caring will be passed on to the care assistants, an 'underclass' on the wards who will be predominantly female with a higher proportion of black people. These issues are not fully addressed in the book. (Another issue which is therefore not addressed is that of middle-class women exploiting lower-class women.)

We agree with much of the authors' analysis of the coexistence of both Fordism and post-Fordism, and the conflict and confusion this creates for workers in the NHS. However, as more recent academic literature on organizations and management point out, conflicting tendencies, contradictions and paradox are 'normal' aspects of work organizations operating in an uncertain and complex world. And workers such as the doctors and managers in this study engage in defence routines and overt as well as covert politicking.

Finally, Walby *et al.* recognize that the cause of the wider structural change has been political. However, we think that this point could have been taken further. What has happened in recent years in the NHS is that politicians have devolved political decisions on to people employed within the health service. In a way it seems that politicians have 'shirked' their responsibilities for the changes they have instigated, and managers, doctors and nurses find themselves accountable for these wider political decisions and become easy scapegoats when things go wrong.

Marie-Claude Foster and Susan F. Murray

Letter

Dear *Feminist Review*

I am glad that there is a letter page in *Feminist Review* now, where readers can give their opinion on the editorial policies of the journal. It was a pleasant surprise to read Christina Griffith's letter in no. 49 (Spring Issue, 1995) as it reminded me of my own reaction to the same issue, 'Sexualities, Challenges and Change': I am referring to Della Grace's lesbian erotic photographs. They reminded me of display windows at strip joints and peep shows found in every big city in the West. How do we know the figures in the photographs are not models who were paid, most probably badly, for the job much in the same way women are employed in the production of peep shows' porn magazines? And even if they are genuine lesbian sadists and masochists, should their display become a necessary part of feminist education for *Feminist Review* readers?

I remember wondering whether *Feminist Review* has any editorial policy over such female representations, which certainly seemed to me out of place in the journal. Sadism and masochism as forms of sexual drives legitimately demand attention from those concerned with the expression of sexuality, but their oppressive and exploitative elements should not be accepted without criticism and questioning. Is it that heterosexual feminists suffer from such guilt about the oppression of lesbians in the past that now, as compensation, they are prepared to bend over backwards to accept all its expressions, including even racism? Ironically, while for heterosexual feminists anything goes as far as lesbian expressions are concerned, quite sharp questioning about oppressive elements in sadistic and masochistic behaviours is coming from the gay community itself.

All I want to say is that accepting differences – sexual or cultural – among women should not amount to becoming *laissez-faire* and reluctant to raise questions of oppression even though no man be involved.

Yours sincerely,

**Rani Drew,
Budapest II,
Szeher ut 47, II/9,
Budapest 1021**

Noticeboard

Call for Papers

Obscure Objects of Desire? – Reviewing the Crafts this Century:
Preliminary Notice and Call for Papers
for a two-day international seminar to be held on 11–12 January 1997 at the University of East Anglia and intended to generate material for a book of essays by various contributors.

In industrialized or industrializing societies craft practice is invariably kept alive by acts of will. This can mean the continuation, or reinvention, of a craft at grass-roots level or a top-down initiative by the state, or by an arm's length agency of the state. A sense of frustrated consumerism, of familiar objects disappearing in a fast changing world, is an important component of the twentieth-century crafts revival, shared by makers and purchasers of craft alike.

In an industrialized, or fast industrializing society, the crafts become 'good to think' – emblematic of a set of desires, ideologies, associations and artistic ambitions. Although this is also true of industrially produced goods (they are certainly objects of desire) their actual facture tends to be of little interest to the consumer. The craft consumer desires not only the object itself but also an understanding of the way in which it is made and, by extension, some sense of intimacy with the maker. Thus in the crafts there is an unusually powerful complicity between maker and consumer.

In the first half of the century only a small, albeit influential, coterie found the crafts 'good for thinking'. But for a movement to succeed it has to touch people's hearts as well as their minds, and attract practitioners and consumers. The relative economic success of the crafts in the 1970s and 1980s in Britain and in the USA reflects the power of the crafts to fulfil people's desires and engage their imagination. On the other hand, the range of goods perceived to be 'crafts' are heterogeneous in the extreme, and might include mass-produced objects, which suggest handwork, or objects which invoke ideas of regionalism but which again might be semi-mass-produced.

The seminar's emphases will in part depend on the response and submission of papers. Possible topics might include:

- the workshop/studio as a site of knowledge
- tools and equipment
- historical precedence and contemporary practice
- relations with design, fine art and architecture and their histories
- relevant European and non-European philosophies
- politics for the crafts
- issues of gender and class
- relations with institutions and counter cultures
- issues of national identity
- the consumption of craft
- projects to theorize the crafts
- the language of craft practice as metaphor.

Papers of 20–30 minutes' duration are invited from writers and researchers in all disciplines. A title and a 150-word outline should be returned to: Tanya Harrod, School of World Art Studies and Museology, University of East Anglia, Norwich NR4 7TJ. Tel: 01603-456161; Fax: 01603-593642. Deadline: 30 May 1996.

Back Issues

1 Women and Revolution in South Yemen, **Molyneux**. Feminist Art Practice, **Davis & Goodal**. Equal Pay and Sex Discrimination, **Snell**. Female Sexuality in Fascist Ideology, **Macciocchi**. Charlotte Brontë's *Shirley*, **Taylor**. Christine Delphy, **Barrett & McIntosh**. OUT OF PRINT.

2 Summer Reading, **O'Rourke**. Disaggregation, **Campaign for Legal and Financial Independence** and **Rights of Women**. The Hayward Annual 1978, **Pollock**. Women and the Cuban Revolution, **Murray**. Matriarchy Study Group Papers, **Lee**. Nurseries in the Second World War, **Riley**.

3 English as a Second Language, **Naish**. Women as a Reserve Army of Labour, **Bruegel**. Chantal Akerman's films, **Martin**. Femininity in the 1950s, **Birmingham Feminist History Group**. On Patriarchy, **Beechey**. Board School Reading Books, **Davin**.

4 Protective Legislation, **Coyle**. Legislation in Israel, **Yuval-Davis**. On 'Beyond the Fragments', **Wilson**. Queen Elizabeth I, **Heisch**. Abortion Politics: **a** dossier. Materialist Feminism, **Delphy**.

5 Feminist Sexual Politics, **Campbell**. Iranian Women, **Tabari**. Women and Power, **Stacey & Price**. Women's Novels, **Coward**. Abortion, **Himmelweit**. Gender and Education, **Nava**. Sybilla Aleramo, **Caesar**. On 'Beyond the Fragments', **Margolis**.

6 'The Tidy House', **Steedman**. Writings on Housework, **Kaluzynska**. The Family Wage, **Land**. Sex and Skill, **Phillips & Taylor**. Fresh Horizons, **Lovell**. Cartoons, **Hay**.

7 Protective Legislation, **Humphries**. Feminists Must Face the Future, **Coultas**. Abortion in Italy, **Caldwell**. Women's Trade Union Conferences, **Breitenbach**. Women's Employment in the Third World, **Elson & Pearson**

8 Socialist Societies Old and New, **Molyneux**. Feminism and the Italian Trade Unions, **Froggett & Torchi**. Feminist Approach to Housing in Britain, **Austerberry & Watson**. Psychoanalysis, **Wilson**. Women in the Soviet Union, **Buckley**. The Struggle within the Struggle, **Kimble**.

9 Position of Women in Family Law, **Brophy & Smart**. Slags or Drags, **Cowie & Lees**. The Ripper and Male Sexuality, **Hollway**. The Material of Male Power, **Cockburn**. Freud's *Dora*, **Moi**. Women in an Iranian Village, **Afshar**. New Office Technology and Women, **Morgall**.

10 Towards a Wages Strategy for Women, **Weir & McIntosh**. Irish Suffrage Movement, **Ward**. A Girls' Project and Some Responses to Lesbianism, **Nava**. The Case for Women's Studies, **Evans**. Equal Pay and Sex Discrimination, **Gregory**. Psychoanalysis and Personal Politics, **Sayers**.

11 Sexuality issue
Sexual Violence and Sexuality, **Coward**. Interview with Andrea Dworkin, **Wilson**. The Dyke, the Feminist and the Devil, **Clark**. Talking Sex, **English, Hollibaugh & Rubin**. Jealousy and Sexual Difference, **Moi**. Ideological Politics 1969–72, **O'Sullivan**. Womanslaughter in the Criminal Law, **Radford**. OUT OF PRINT.

12 ANC Women's Struggles, **Kimble & Unterhalter**. Women's Strike in Holland 1981, **de Bruijn & Henkes**. Politics of Feminist Research, **McRobbie**. Khomeini's Teachings on Women, **Afshar**. Women in the Labour Party 1906–1920, **Rowan**. Documents from the Indian Women's Movement, **Gothoskar & Patel**.

13 Feminist Perspectives on Sport, **Graydon**. Patriarchal Criticism and Henry James, **Kappeler**. The Barnard Conference on Sexuality, **Wilson**. Danger and Pleasure in Nineteenth Century Feminist Sexual Thought, **Gordon & Du Bois**. Anti-Porn: Soft Issue, Hard World, **Rich**. Feminist Identity and Poetic Tradition, **Montefiore**.

14 Femininity and its Discontents, **Rose**. Inside and Outside Marriage, **Gittins**. The Pro-family Left in the United States, **Epstein & Ellis**. Women's Language and Literature, **McKluskie**. The Inevitability of Theory, **Fildes**. The 150 Hours in Italy, **Caldwell**. Teaching Film, **Clayton**.

15 Women's Employment, **Beechey**. Women and Trade Unions, **Charles**. Lesbianism and Women's Studies, **Adamson**. Teaching Women's Studies at Secondary School, **Kirton**. Gender, Ethnic and Class Divisions, **Anthias & Yuval-Davis**. Women Studying or Studying Women, **Kelly & Pearson**. Girls, Jobs and Glamour, **Sherratt**. Contradictions in Teaching Women's Studies, **Phillips & Hurstfield**.

16 Romance Fiction, Female Sexuality and Class, **Light**. The White Brothel, **Kappeler**. Sadomasochism and Feminism, **France**. Trade Unions and Socialist Feminism, **Cockburn**. Women's Movement and the Labour Party, **Interview with Labour Party Feminists**. Feminism and 'The Family', **Caldwell**.

17 Many voices, one chant: black feminist perspectives
Challenging Imperial Feminism, **Amos & Parmar**. Black Women, the Economic Crisis and the British State, **Mama**. Asian Women in the Making of History, **Trivedi**. Black Lesbian Discussions, **Carmen, Gail, Shaila & Pratibha**. Poetry. Black Women Organizing Autonomously: a collection.

18 Cultural politics
Writing with Women. A Metaphorical Journey, **Lomax**. Karen Alexander: Video Worker, **Nava**. Poetry by **Riley, Whiteson** and **Davies**. Women's Films, **Montgomery**. 'Correct Distance' a photo-text, **Tabrizian**. Julia Kristeva on Femininity, **Jones**. Feminism and the Theatre, **Wandor**. Alexis Hunter, **Osborne**. Format Photographers, Dear Linda, **Kuhn**.

19 The Female Nude in the work of Suzanne Valadon, **Betterton**. Refuges for Battered Women, **Pahl**. Thin is the Feminist Issue, **Diamond**. New Portraits for Old, **Martin & Spence**.

20 Prisonhouses, **Steedman**. Ethnocentrism and Socialist Feminism, **Barrett & McIntosh**. What Do Women Want? **Rowbotham**. Women's Equality and the European Community, **Hoskyns**. Feminism and the Popular Novel of the 1890s, **Clarke**.

21 Going Private: The Implications of Privatization for Women's Work, **Coyle**. A Girl Needs to Get Street-wise: Magazines for the 1980s, **Winship**. Family Reform in Socialist States: The Hidden Agenda, **Molyneux**. Sexual Segregation in the Pottery Industry, **Sarsby**.

22 Interior Portraits: Women, Physiology and the Male Artist, **Pointon**. The Control of Women's Labour: The Case of Homeworking, **Allen & Wolkowitz**. Homeworking: Time for Change, **Cockpit Gallery & Londonwide Homeworking Group**. Feminism and Ideology: The Terms of Women's Stereotypes, **Seiter**. Feedback: Feminism and Racism, **Ramazanoglu, Kazi, Lees, Safia Mirza**.

23 Socialist-feminism: out of the blue
Feminism and Class Politics: A Round-Table Discussion, **Barrett, Campbell, Philips, Weir & Wilson**. Upsetting an Applecart: Difference, Desire and Lesbian Sadomasochism, **Ardill & O'Sullivan**. Armagh and Feminist Strategy, **Loughran**. Transforming Socialist-Feminism: The Challenge of Racism, **Bhavnani & Coulson**. Socialist-Feminists and Greenham, **Finch & Hackney Greenham Groups**. Socialist-Feminism and the Labour Party: Some Experiences from Leeds, **Perrigo**. Some Political Implications of Women's Involvement in the Miners' Strike 1984–85, **Rowbotham & McCrindle**. Sisterhood: Political Solidarity Between Women, **Hooks**. European Forum of Socialist-Feminists, **Lees & McIntosh**. Report from Nairobi, **Hendessi**.

24 Women Workers in New Industries in Britain, **Glucksmann**. The Relationship of Women to Pornography, **Bower**. The Sex Discrimination Act 1975, **Atkins**. The Star Persona of Katharine Hepburn, **Thumim**.

25 Difference: A Special Third World Women Issue, **Minh-ha**. Melanie Klein, Psychoanalysis and Feminism, **Sayers**. Rethinking Feminist Attitudes Towards Mothering, **Gieve**. EEOC v. Sears, Roebuck and Company: A Personal Account, **Kessler-Harris**. Poems, **Wood**. Academic Feminism and the Process of Deradicalization, **Currie & Kazi**. A Lover's Distance: A Photoessay, **Boffin**.

26 Resisting Amnesia: Feminism, Painting and Post-Modernism, **Lee**. The Concept of Difference, **Barrett**. The Weary Sons of Freud, **Clément**. Short Story, **Cole**. Taking the Lid Off: Socialist Feminism in Oxford, **Collette**. For and Against the European Left: Socialist Feminists Get Organized, **Benn**. Women and the State: A Conference of Feminist Activists, **Weir**.

27 Women, feminism and the third term
Women and Income Maintenance, **Lister**. Women in the Public Sector, **Phillips**. Can Feminism Survive a Third Term?, **Loach**. Sex in Schools, **Wolpe**. Carers and the Careless, **Doyal**. Interview with Diane Abbott, **Segal**. The Problem With No Name: Re-reading Friedan, **Bowlby**. Second Thoughts on the Second Wave, **Rosenfelt & Stacey**. Nazi Feminists?, **Gordon**.

28 Family secrets: child sexual abuse
Introduction to an Issue: Family Secrets as Public Drama, **McIntosh**. Challenging the Orthodoxy: Towards a Feminist Theory and Practice, **MacLeod & Saraga**. The Politics of Child Sexual Abuse: Notes from American History, **Gordon**. What's in a Name?: Defining Child Sexual Abuse, **Kelly**. A Case, **Anon**. Defending Innocence: Ideologies of Childhood, **Kitzinger**. Feminism and the Seductiveness of the 'Real Event', **Scott**. Cleveland and the Press: Outrage and Anxiety in the Reporting of Child Sexual Abuse, **Nava**. Child Sexual Abuse and the Law, **Woodcraft**. Poem, **Betcher**. Brixton Black Women's Centre: Organizing on Child Sexual Abuse, **Bogle**. Bridging the Gap: Glasgow Women's Support Project, **Bell & MacLeod**. Claiming Our Status as Experts: Community Organizing, **Norwich Consultants on Sexual Violence**. Islington Social Services: Developing a Policy on Child Sexual Abuse, **Boushel & Noakes**. Developing a Feminist School Policy on Child Sexual Abuse, **O'Hara**. 'Putting Ideas into their Heads': Advising the Young, **Mills**. Child Sexual Abuse Crisis Lines: Advice for Our British Readers.

29 Abortion: the international agenda
Whatever Happened to 'A Woman's Right to Choose'?, **Berer**. More than 'A Woman's Right to Choose'?, **Himmelweit**. Abortion in the Republic of Ireland, **Barry**. Across the Water, **Irish Women's Abortion Support Group**. Spanish Women and the Alton Bill, **Spanish Women's Abortion Support Group**. The Politics of Abortion in Australia: Freedom, Church and State, **Coleman**. Abortion in Hungary, **Szalai**. Women and Population Control in China: Issues of Sexuality, Power and Control, **Hillier**. The Politics of Abortion in Nicaragua: Revolutionary Pragmatism –

or Feminism in the Realm of Necessity?, **Molyneux**. Who Will Sing for Theresa?, **Bernstein**. She's Gotta Have It: The Representation of Black Female Sexuality on Film, **Simmonds**. Poems, **Gallagher**. Dyketactics for Difficult Times: A Review of the 'Homosexuality, Which Homosexuality?' Conference, **Franklin & Stacey**.

30 Capital, gender and skill

Women Homeworkers in Rural Spain, **Lever**. Fact and Fiction: George Egerton and Nellie Shaw, **Butler**. Feminist Political Organization in Iceland: Some Reflections on the Experience of Kwenna Frambothid, **Dominelli & Jonsdottir**. Under Western Eyes: Feminist Scholarship and Colonial Discourses, **Talpade Mohanty**. Bedroom Horror: The Fatal Attraction of *Intercourse,* **Merck**. AIDS: Lessons from the Gay Community, **Patton**. Poems, **Agbabi**.

31 The past before us: 20 years of feminism

Slow Change or No Change?: Feminism, Socialism and the Problem of Men, **Segal**. There's No Place Like Home: On the Place of Identity in Feminist Politics, **Adams**. New Alliances: Socialist-Feminism in the Eighties, **Harriss**. Other Kinds of Dreams, **Parmar**. Complexity, Activism, Optimism: Interview with **Angela Y. Davis**. To Be or Not To Be: The Dilemmas of Mothering, **Rowbotham**. Seizing Time and Making New: Feminist Criticism, Politics and Contemporary Feminist Fiction, **Lauret**. Lessons from the Women's Movement in Europe, **Haug**. Women in Management, **Coyle**. Sex in the Summer of '88, **Ardill & O'Sullivan**. Younger Women and Feminism, **Hobsbawm & Macpherson**. Older Women and Feminism, **Stacey; Curtis; Summerskill**.

32

'Those Who Die for Life Cannot Be Called Dead': Women and Human Rights Protest in Latin America, **Schirmer**. Violence Against Black Women: Gender, Race and State Responses, **Mama**. Sex and Race in the Labour Market, **Breugel**. The 'Dark Continent': Africa as Female Body in Haggard's Adventure Fiction, **Stott**. Gender, Class and the Welfare State: the Case of Income Security in Australia, **Shaver**. Ethnic Feminism: Beyond the Pseudo-Pluralists, **Gorelick**.

33

Restructuring the Woman Question: *Perestroika* and Prostitution, **Waters**. Contemporary Indian Feminism, **Kumar**. 'A Bit On the Side'?: Gender Struggles in South Africa, **Beall, Hassim and Todes**. 'Young Bess': Historical Novels and Growing Up, **Light**. Madeline Pelletier (1874–1939): The Politics of Sexual Oppression, **Mitchell**.

34 Perverse politics: lesbian issues

Pat Parker: a tribute, **Brimstone**. International Lesbianism: Letter from São Paulo, **Rodrigues**; Israel, **Pittsburgh**, Italy, **Fiocchetto**. The De-eroticization of Women's Liberation: Social Purity Movements and the Revolutionary Feminism of Sheila Jeffreys, **Hunt**. Talking About It: Homophobia in the Black Community, **Gomez & Smith**. Lesbianism and the Labour Party, **Tobin**. Skirting the Issue: Lesbian Fashion for the 1990s, **Blackman & Perry**. Butch/Femme Obsessions, **Ardill & O'Sullivan**. Archives: The Will to Remember, **Nestle**; International Archives, **Read**. Audre Lorde: Vignettes and Mental Conversations, **Lewis**. Lesbian Tradition,

Field. Mapping: Lesbians, AIDS and Sexuality: An Interview with Cindy Patton, **O'Sullivan**. Significant Others: Lesbians and Psychoanalytic Theory, **Hamer**. The Pleasure Threshold: Looking at Lesbian Pornography on Film, **Smyth**. Cartoon, **Charlesworth**. Voyages of the Valkyries: Recent Lesbian Pornographic Writing, **Dunn**.

35 Campaign Against Pornography, **Norden**. The Mothers' Manifesto and Disputes over 'Mutterlichkeit', **Chamberlayne**. Multiple Mediations: Feminist Scholarship in the Age of Multi-National Reception, **Mani**. Cagney and Lacey Revisited, **Alcock & Robson**. Cutting a Dash: The Dress of Radclyffe Hall and Una Troubridge, **Rolley**. Deviant Dress, **Wilson**. The House that Jill Built: Lesbian Feminist Organizing in Toronto, 1976–1980, **Ross**. Women in Professional Engineering: the Interaction of Gendered Structures and Values, **Carter & Kirkup**. Identity Politics and the Hierarchy of Oppression, **Briskin**. Poetry: **Bufkin, Zumwalt**.

36 'The Trouble Is It's Ahistorical': The Problem of the Unconscious in Modern Feminist Theory, **Minsky**. Feminism and Pornography, **Ellis, O'Dair and Tallmer**. Who Watches the Watchwomen? Feminists Against Censorship, **Rodgerson & Semple**. Pornography and Violence: What the 'Experts' Really Say, **Segal**. The Woman In My Life: Photography of Women, **Nava**. Splintered Sisterhood: Antiracism in a Young Women's Project, **Connolly**. Woman, Native, Other, **Parmar** interviews **Trinh T. Minh-ha**. Out But Not Down: Lesbians' Experience of Housing, **Edgerton**. Poems: **Evans Davies, Toth, Weinbaum**. Oxford Twenty Years On: Where Are We Now?, **Gamman & O'Neill**. The Embodiment of Ugliness and the Logic of Love: The Danish Redstockings Movement, **Walter**.

37 **Theme issue: Women, religion and dissent**
Black Women, Sexism and Racism: Black or Antiracist Feminism?, **Tang Nain**. Nursing Histories: Reviving Life in Abandoned Selves, **McMahon**. The Quest for National Identity: Women, Islam and the State of Bangladesh, **Kabeer**. Born Again Moon: Fundamentalism in Christianity and the Feminist Spirituality Movement, **McCrickard**. Washing our Linen: One Year of Women Against Fundamentalism, **Connolly**. **Siddiqui** on *Letter to Christendom*, **Bard** on *Generations of Memories*, **Patel** on *Women Living Under Muslim Laws Dossiers 1–6*, Poem, **Kay**. More Cagney and Lacey, **Gamman**.

38 The Modernist Style of Susan Sontag, **McRobbie**. Tantalizing Glimpses of Stolen Glances: Lesbians Take Photographs, **Fraser and Boffin**. Reflections on the Women's Movement in Trinidad, **Mohammed**. Fashion, Representation and Femininity, **Evans & Thornton**. The European Women's Lobby, **Hoskyns**. Hendessi on *Law of Desire: Temporary Marriage in Iran*, **Kaveney** on *Mercy*.

39 **Shifting territories: feminism & Europe**
Between Hope and Helplessness: Women in the GDR, **Dölling**. Where Have All the Women Gone? Women and the Women's Movement in East Central Europe, **Einborn**. The End of Socialism in Europe – A New Challenge For Socialist Feminism?, **Haug**. The Second 'No': Women in Hungary, **Kiss**. The Citizenship

Debate: Women, the State and Ethnic Processes, **Yuval-Davis**. Fortress Europe and Migrant Women, **Morokvasíc**. Racial Equality and 1992, **Dummett**. Questioning *Perestroika*: A Socialist Feminist Interrogation, **Pearson**. Postmodernism and its Discontents, **Soper**. Feminists and Socialism: After the Cold War, **Kaldor**. Socialism Out of the Common Pots, **Mitter**. 1989 and All That, **Campbell**. In Listening Mode, **Cockburn**. **Women in Action: Country by Country:** The Soviet Union; Yugoslavia; Czechoslovakia; Hungary; Poland. **Reports:** International Gay and Lesbian Association: Black Women and Europe 1992.

40 Fleurs du Mal or Second-Hand Roses?: Nathalie Barney, Romaine Brooks, and the 'Originality of the Avant-Garde', **Elliott & Wallace**. Poem, **Tyler-Bennett**. Feminism and Motherhood: An American 'Reading', **Snitow**. Qualitative Research, Appropriation of the 'Other' and Empowerment, **Opie**. Disabled Women and the Feminist Agenda, **Begum**. Postcard From the Edge: Thoughts on the 'Feminist Theory: An International Debate' Conference at Glasgow University, July 1991, **Radstone**. Review Essay, **Munt**.

41 Editorial. The Selling of HRT: Playing on the Fear Factor, **Worcester & Whatley**. The Cancer Drawings of Catherine Arthur, **Sebastyen**. Ten years of Women's Health 1982–92, **James**. AIDS Activism: Women and AIDS activism in Victoria, Australia, **Mitchell**. A Woman's Subject, **Friedli**. HIV and the Invisibility of Women: Is there a Need to Redefine AIDS?, **Scharf & Toole**. Lesbians Evolving Health Care: Cancer and AIDS, **Winnow**. Now is the Time for Feminist Criticism: A Review of *Asinimali!*, **Steinberg**. Ibu or the Beast?: Gender Interests in Two Indonesian Women's Organizations, **Wieringa**. Reports on Motherlands: Symposium on African, Caribbean and Asian Women's Writing, **Smart**. The European Forum of Socialist Feminists, **Bruegel**. Review Essay, **Gamman**.

42 Feminist fictions
Editorial. Angela Carter's *The Bloody Chamber* and the Decolonization of Feminine Sexuality, **Makinen**. Feminist Writing: Working with Women's Experience, **Haug**. Three Aspects of Sex in Marge Piercy's *Fly Away Home*, **Hauser**. Are They Reading Us? Feminist Teenage Fiction, **Bard**. Sexuality in Lesbian Romance Fiction, **Hermes**. A Psychoanalytic Account for Lesbianism, **Castendyk**. Mary Wollstonecraft and the Problematic of Slavery, **Ferguson**. Reviews.

43 Issues for feminism
Family, Motherhood and Zulu Nationalism: the Politics of the Inkatha Women's Brigade, **Hassim**. Postcolonial Feminism and the Veil: Thinking the Difference, **Abu Odeh**. Feminism, the Menopause and Hormone Replacement Therapy, **Lewis**. Feminism and Disability, **Morris**. 'What is Pornography?': An Analysis of the Policy Statement of the Campaign Against Pornography and Censorship, **Smith**. Reviews.

44 Nationalisms and national identities
Women, Nationalism and Islam in Contemporary Political Discourse in Iran, **Yeganeh**. Feminism, Citizenship and National Identity, **Curthoys**. Remapping

and Renaming: New Cartographies of Identity, Gender and Landscape in Ireland, **Nash**. Rap Poem: Easter 1991, **Medbh**. Family Feuds: Gender, Nationalism and the Family, **McClintock**. Women as Activists; Women as Symbols: A Study of the Indian Nationalist Movement, **Thapar**. Gender, Nationalisms and National Identities: Bellagio Symposium Report, **Hall**. Culture or Citizenship? Notes from the Gender and Colonialism Conference, Galway, Ireland, May 1992, **Connolly**. Reviews.

45 Thinking through ethnicities

Audre Lorde: Reflections. Re-framing Europe: Engendered Racisms, Ethnicities and Nationalisms in Contemporary Western Europe, **Brah**. Towards a Multicultural Europe? 'Race' Nation and Identity in 1992 and Beyond, **Bhavnani**. Another View: Photo Essay, **Pollard**. Growing Up White: Feminism, Racism and the Social Geography of Childhood, **Frankenberg**. Poem, **Kay**. Looking Beyond the Violent Break-up of Yugoslavia, **Coulson**. Personal Reactions of a Bosnian Woman to the War in Bosnia, **Harper**. Serbian Nationalism: Nationalism of My Own People, **Korac**. Belgrade Feminists 1992: Separation, Guilt and Identity Crisis, **Mladjenovic** and **Litricin**. Report on a Council of Europe Minority Youth Committee Seminar on Sexism and Racism in Western Europe, **Walker**. Reviews.

46 Sexualities: challenge and change

Chips, Coke and Rock-'n-Roll: Children's Mediation of an Invitation to a First Dance Party, **Rossiter**. Power and Desire: The Embodiment of Female Sexuality, **Holland, Ramazanoglu, Sharpe, Thomson**. Two Poems, **Janzen**. A Girton Girl on the Throne: Queen Christina and Versions of Lesbianism 1906–1933. Changing Interpretations of the Sexuality of Queen Christina of Sweden, **Waters**. The Pervert's Progress: An Analysis of 'The Story of O' and The Beauty Trilogy, **Ziv**. Dis-Graceful Images: Della Grace and Lesbian Sadomasochism, **Lewis**. Reviews.

47

Virgin Territories and Motherlands: Colonial and Nationalist Representations of Africa, **Innes**. The Impact of the Islamic Movement in Egypt, **Shukrallah**. Mothering on the Lam: Politics, Gender Fantasies and Maternal Thinking in Women Associated with Armed, Clandestine Organizations in the US, **Zwerman**. Treading the Traces of Discarded History: Photo-Essay, **Marchant**. The Feminist Production of Knowledge: Is Deconstruction a Practice for Women?, **Nash**. 'Divided We Stand': Sex, Gender and Sexual Difference, **Moore**. Reviews.

48 Sex and the state

Editorial. Not Just (Any) *Body* Can be a Citizen: The Politics of Law, Sexuality and Postcoloniality in Trinidad and Tobago and the Bahamas, **Alexander**. State, Family and Personal Responsibility: The Changing Balance for Lone Mothers in the United Kingdom, **Millar**. Moral Rhetoric and Public Health Pragmatism: The Recent Politics of Sex Education, **Thomson**. Through the Parliamentary Looking Glass: 'Real' and 'Pretend' Families in Contemporary British Politics, **Reinhold**. In Search of Gender Justice: Sexual Assault and the Criminal Justice System, **Gregory and Lees**. God's Bullies: Attacks on Abortion, **Hadley**. Sex Work, HIV and the State: an Interview with Nel Druce, **Overs**. Reviews.

49 Feminist politics – Colonial/postcolonial worlds

Women on the March: Right-Wing Mobilization in Contemporary India, **Mazumdar**. Colonial Encounters in Late-Victorian England: Pandita Ramabai at Cheltenham and Wantage, **Burton**. Subversive Intent: A Social Theory of Gender, **Maharaj**. My Discourse/My Self: Therapy as Possibility (for women who eat compulsively), **Hopwood**. Poems, **Donohue**. Review Essays. Reviews.

50 The Irish issue: the British question

Editorial. Deconstructing Whiteness: Irish Women in Britain, **Hickman and Walter**. Poem, **Smyth**. States of Change: Reflections of Ireland in Several Uncertain Parts, **Smyth**. Silences: Irish Women and Abortion, **Fletcher**. Poem, **Higgins**. Irish Women Poets and the Iconic Feminine, **Mills**. Irish/Woman/Artwork: Selective Readings, **Robinson**. Self-Determination: The Republican Feminist Agenda, **Hackett**. Ourselves Alone? Clár na mBan Conference Report, **Connolly**. Conflicting Interests: The British and Irish Suffrage Movements, **Ward**. Women Disarmed: The Militarization of Politics in Ireland 1913–23, **Benton**. 'The Crying Game', **Edge**.

51 In Love with Inspector Morse

Beleagured but Determined: Irish Women Writers in Irish, **Harris**. In Love with Inspector Morse: Feminist Subculture and Quality Television, **Thomas**. Great Expectations: Rehabilitating the Recalcitrant War Poets, **Plain**. Creating a Space for Absent Voices: Disabled Women's Experience of Receiving Assistance with their Daily Living Activities, **Morris**. Imagining (the) Difference: Gender Ethnicity and Metaphors of Nation, **Molloy**. Poems, **Sharp**.

52 The World Turned Upside Down: Feminisms in the Antipodes

The Curse of the Smile: Ambivalence and the Asian Woman in Australian Multiculturalism, **Ang**. Unravelling Identities: Performance and Criticism in Australian Feminisms, **Genovese**. Feminism and Sexual Abuse: Troubled Thoughts on Some New Zealand Issues, **Guy**. Negotiating the Politics of Inclusion: Women and Australian Labor Governments 1983–95, **Johnson**. Women I Kat Raet Long Human Raet O No? Women's Rights, Human Rights and Domestic Violence in Vanuatu, **Jolly**. 'Warmth and Unity With All Women?' Historicizing Racism in the Australian Women's Movement, **Murdolo**. Women Mail Order Brides and Boys' Own Tales: Representations of Asian Australian Marriages, **Robinson**. Gender, Metaphor and the State, **Sawer**. Feminism and Institutionalized Racism: Inclusion and Exclusion at an Australian Feminist Refuge, **Wilson**.

Feminist Review was founded in 1979. Since that time it has established itself as one of the UK's leading feminist journals.

• Why not subscribe? Make sure of your copy

All subscriptions run in calendar years. The issues for 1996 are Nos. 52, 53 and 54. You will save over £5 pa on the single copy price.

• Subscription rates, 1996 (3 issues)

Individual Subscriptions
UK/EEC	£28
Overseas	£28
North America	$44

A number of reduced cost (£20 per year: UK only) subscriptions are available for readers experiencing financial hardship, e.g. unemployed, student, low-paid. If you'd like to be considered for a reduced subscription, please write to the Collective, c/o the Feminist Review office, 52 Featherstone Street, London EC1Y 8RT.

Institutional Subscriptions
UK	£75	Single Issues	£10.99
Overseas	£82		
North America	$120		

☐ Please send me one year's subscription to **Feminist Review**
☐ Please send me _____ copies of back issue no. _____

METHOD OF PAYMENT
☐ I enclose a cheque/international money order to the value of _____
   made payable to Routledge Journals
☐ Please charge my Access/Visa/American Express/Diners Club account

Account no. ☐☐☐☐☐☐☐☐☐☐☐☐☐☐☐☐

Expiry date _____ Signature _____

If the address below is different from the registered address of your credit card, please give your registered address separately.
PLEASE USE BLOCK CAPITALS
Name _____
Address _____
_____
_____ Postcode _____
☐ Please send me a Routledge Journals Catalogue
☐ Please send me a Routledge Gender and Women's Studies Catalogue

Please return this form with payment to:
Routledge Subscriptions Department, Cheriton House, North Way, Andover, Hants SP10 5BE

Womanist and Feminist Aesthetics

A Comparative Review
Tuzyline Jita Allan

Alice Walker's womanist theory about black feminist identity and practice also contains a critique of white liberal feminism. This is the first in-depth study to examine issues of identity within feminism by drawing on Walker's notion of an essential black feminist consciousness.

Allan defines womanism as a "(r)evolutionary aesthetic that seeks to fully realize the feminist goal of resistance to patriarchal domination," demonstrated most powerfully in *The Color Purple*. She also recognizes the complexities and ambiguities embedded in the concept, particularly the notion of a fixed and unitary black feminist identity, separate and distinct from its white counterpart. Woolf's *Mrs Dalloway* and Drabble's *The Middle Ground*, she argues, do not allay Walker's concerns about white liberal feminist practice, but they reveal signs of struggle that complicate the womanist/feminist dichotomy. Emecheta's *The Joys of Motherhood*, an ostensibly womanist text, fails to fit the race-restrictive womanist paradigm, and Walker's own aesthetic trajectory—before *The Color Purple*—place her outside womanist boundaries. Finally, Allan's intertextual reading reveals significant commonalities and differences.

In the current debate among competing feminisms, this critical appraisal of womanist theory underscores the need for new thinking about essentialism, identity, and difference, and also for creative cooperation in the struggle against domination.

Tuzyline Jita Allan, originally from Sierra Leone, West Africa, teaches in the English Department at Baruch College of the City University of New York.
175 pages, bibliog, index, **£15.95 paper**

OHIO UNIVERSITY PRESS
AUPG, 1 Gower Street, London WC1E 6HA Tel: (0171) 580 3994

CHANGING SEX
Transsexualism, Technology, and the Idea of Gender
Bernice L. Hausman
"*Changing Sex* makes a landmark contribution to gender studies and the understanding of transsexualism. It is original, provocative, and will be controversial in the best sense."
—Julia Epstein, Haverford College
320pp, 17 b&w photos, £16.95 pb

ANIMALS AND WOMEN
Feminist Theoretical Explorations
Carol J. Adams and Josephine Donovan, editors
Offering a feminist perspective on the status of animals, this unique volume argues persuasively that both the social construction and oppressions of women are inextricably connected to the ways in which we comprehend and abuse other species. 360pp, £15.95 pb

SKIN SHOWS
Gothic Horror and the Technology of Monsters
Judith Halberstam
"*Skin Shows* is the Gothic book that many of us have been waiting for, and it is every bit as smart as we had hoped it would be. The results are dazzling."
—George E. Haggerty, University of California
240pp, 6 b&w photos, £14.95 pb

BAD OBJECTS
Essays Popular and Unpopular
Naomi Schor
"This is an impressive volume of elegant essays that will confirm Schor's reputation as one of feminism's finest scholars, and one of the most expansive and precise minds in French studies."—Judith Butler
232pp, £14.95 pb

TECHNOLOGIES OF THE GENDERED BODY
Reading Cyborg Women
Anne Balsamo
"Balsamo takes us further into cyborg territory than any intelligent book has done."—Andrew Ross
272pp, 29 b&w photos, £16.95 pb

THE BODY IN LATE-CAPITALIST USA
Donald M. Lowe
"Lowe has produced an impressive argument about the transformation of the body in recent society. He presents in lucid prose a complex argument for a revised Marxism in conjunction with various poststructuralist positions as the basis for a new analysis of contemporary capitalism." —Mark Poster
224pp, £14.95 pb

TROUBLED BODIES
Critical Perspectives on Postmodernism, Medical Ethics, and the Body
Paul A. Komesaroff, editor
"*Troubled Bodies* presents an excellent introduction to the philosophical and cultural settings of a postmodern medical ethics."—Mark Seltzer, Cornell University
296pp, £15.95 pb

AIDS TV
Identity, Community, and Alternative Video
Alexandra Juhasz
With a Videography by Catherine Saalfield
"[*AIDS TV*] combines broad social analysis and a culturally informed feminist politics with the work of producing AIDS video."—Paula Treichler, coeditor of *Cultural Studies*
352pp, 22 b&w illus., £16.95 pb

DUKE UNIVERSITY PRESS, AUPG, 1 Gower St., London WC1E 6HA (0171) 580 3994

Rape on Trial
How the Mass Media Construct Legal Reform and Social Change
Lisa M. Cuklanz
Why has so much of the public discussion of rape focused on a few specific cases, and to what extent has this discussion incorporated the feminist perspective on rape? This volume explores these questions and provides answers based on a detailed examination of the mainstream news coverage and subsequent fictionalized representations of three highly publicized trials in the U.S. from the period between 1978 and 1988.
160pp, £27.50hb, £11.95pb

Choosing Unsafe Sex
AIDS-Risk Denial Among Disadvantaged Women
E. J. Sobo
In an effort to explain why the AIDS education programs have failed to stop clients from practicing unsafe sex, *Choosing Unsafe Sex* explores the links between women's condom use rate and their experiences and understandings of heterosexual relationships. It will be of interest to all who seek a deeper understanding of mainstream assumptions about heterosexual relationships.
256pp, 10 tables, £13.95pb, £32.95hb

Sick and Tired of Being Sick and Tired
Black Women's Health Activism in America, 1890-1950
Susan L. Smith
This book—the first full-scale examination of the public health initiatives created by African Americans—argues that health reform was a cornerstone of early black civil rights activity in the United States. In an era of legalized segregation, health improvement was tied to the struggle for social change. 288pp, £15.95 pb

Television Culture and Women's Lives
thirtysomething and the Contradictions of Gender
Margaret J. Heide
Contemporary cultural theory, feminist criticism, and ethnography converge in this provocative study of the construction of meaning in mass culture. Heide explores the complex relationship between the gender conflicts played out in the scripts of the popular television show *thirtysomething* and the real-life conflicts experienced by "baby-boomer" women viewers. Heide challenges theories that viewers passively absorb mass media messages.
192pp, £27.50hb, £11.95pb

Family Plots
The De-Oedipalization of Popular Culture
Dana Heller
This book traces the fault lines of the Freudian family romance and holds that although the family itself is nowhere the "family plot" is very much alive in post-World War II American culture. Interrogating the authority of family master narratives in contemporary culture and drawing from current literary, cultural, and media studies; feminist and lesbian and gay theory; and research on changing structures of the family in the postwar era, Heller argues that the very idea of "family" is an arena of conflict and struggle over the limits of private and public discourse.
248pp, £32.95hb, £13.95pb

University of Pennsylvania Press
Academic & University Publishers Group
1 Gower Street, London WC1E 6HA
Tel: (0171) 580 3994